John Deere Industrials

Brian Rukes

MBI Publishing Company

First published in 2002 by MBI Publishing Company, Galtier Plaza, Suite 200, 380 Jackson Street, St. Paul, MN 55101-3885 USA

MBI Publishing Company books are also available at discounts in bulk quantity for industrial or sales-promotional use. For details write to Special Sales Manager at Motorbooks International Wholesalers & Distributors, Galtier Plaza, Suite 200, 380 Jackson Street, St. Paul, MN 55101-3885 USA.

Library of Congress Cataloging-in-Publication Data Available

ISBN 0-7603-1023-8

On the front cover:
Model D. *Andy Kraushaar*

On the frontispiece:
1956 Deere trademark logo.

On the title page:
Model MC. *Andy Kraushaar*

On the back cover:
top: Model MI. *Randy Leffingwell*

bottom left: In 2001, Deere & Company had as many as six motor grader models in production.

bottom right: Model 440. *Deere & Company Archives*

Edited by Kris Palmer
Designed by Dan Perry

Printed in Hong Kong

CONTENTS

ACKNOWLEDGMENTS

Writing this book has been a tremendous discovery process, and it could not have been finished without the grace of God and the assistance and encouragement of many, many people.

First off, I thank the people at Deere & Company Archives for assisting me in finding the information needed for this book. I particularly thank Mr. Leslie Stegh, the head archivist at Deere Archives, for his insight, assistance, and unending enthusiasm regarding Deere & Company history. I would also like to extend a special thank-you to Lynn Timmerman at the John Deere Collectors' Center for granting me access to Deere archives.

I would also like to extend a hearty thanks to Mr. Brian R. Alm for helping me with information for this book. Mr. Alm worked for Deere for a number of years and was quite familiar with the company and its industrial programs. I thank Mr. Alm for his insights and for allowing me to use information from his book, *A History of the John Deere Industrial Equipment Division*, and direct quotes therefrom for this book.

Next, I would like to thank all those who assisted me in one way or another with photography for this book. I extend an emphatic, heartfelt "Thank You!" to Randy Leffingwell for graciously providing me with some of his photos for use in this book. I also would like to thank Andy Kraushaar for allowing me to use some of his photos as well, including the cover photo. Additionally, I thank all of those who allowed me to photograph their tractors or provided me with more information for the book. These include the people at John Deere industrial dealer C.L. Boyd in Oklahoma City; Harry, Mike, and Viola Martens; and Clarence J. VonTungeln, among others. Thank you all.

I also sincerely thank all of those people who were close to me while I was compiling this book. Two I appreciate perhaps most are my grandmother, LaVerne Crumley, and my father, Charles Rukes; both helped me get through all the difficult times I had in the several months I was working on this book. They showed me that they cared more than I could ever have hoped for, and they put up with a lot from me in that time, including calls at midnight or 2 AM. I also thank Dad for supplying me with some of the information I needed regarding how some of these machines work. Dad, a veteran heavy-equipment operator, has spent many hours at the controls of road graders and bulldozers alike, and I greatly value his insight and knowledge. Furthermore, if it weren't for Dad, I probably never would have gotten interested in tractors and machinery as much as I have. Dad, I cherish the memories of riding on the armrest of your dozer when you were building that one pond on our place. All the times of coming back to the house hard of hearing afterwards (and consequently getting Mom a bit upset) were worth it! Thanks, Dad.

I also want to thank a wonderful friend of mine who helped instill in me a sense of belonging, purpose, and true worth in the last month and a half I was working on this book. I hadn't seen her in several years—since sixth grade, in fact—but I finally found her again in a great hour of need. You know who you are. Thank you so very much.

I would also like to thank all of my friends at church, at Southwestern Oklahoma State University here in Weatherford, and in the tractor-collecting community throughout the world. My thanks also go to the folks at MBI Publishing Company whom I worked with on this book, including editor Sara Perfetti and former MBI editor John Adams-Graf. Both of them showed a tremendous interest in my work and gave me a great deal of insight as to how to proceed with this book. Thank you all for all you've done.

I can say with certainty that I will be extremely pleased when I see this book finally get to print. It has been a challenge, but I have weathered the storm, thanks to God and to all of you whom I mentioned here (and likely some I failed to mention). I don't think any book I ever will write could ever be as special to me as the first book I ever had published, but this one comes close. I hope every one of you enjoys it.

INTRODUCTION

John Deere is a brand name that people from around the world know by name and by sight. John Deere has of course become synonymous with farming—even people who have never even seen a farm know that John Deere makes tractors. And, believe it or not, some people actually think that John Deere is the only brand of tractor currently being produced! Furthermore, when people hear the John Deere name today, their thoughts often turn to things besides the merely agricultural—they think of lawn and grounds care products, they think of utility vehicles, and they think of industrial machinery. But things haven't always been that way.

When John Deere the man started producing his steel plows in Grand Detour, Illinois, in the year 1837, he had no idea how influential his company would be to the agricultural world in the years to come. And, for decades after Deere started his company, the John Deere name usually evoked responses only from those people familiar with or involved in agriculture. Farmers recognized the brand for what it produced, which was then "Quality Farm Implements" (one of the trademark terms used by the company). And when Deere & Company started producing tractors, the company didn't waver at all in its dedication to produce dependable, high-quality, lasting products. That dedication persists to this day.

When John Deere the company started producing tractors, it firmly established itself as one of the greatest full-line farm machinery companies of all time. And farmers quickly went from recognizing John Deere as a producer of sound agricultural implements to a producer of sound agricultural machines, tractors included. And, by 1935, nearly 100 years after John Deere the man started producing his steel plows, the image of the John Deere plow was no longer the first thing that popped into most farmers' minds when they heard the name. Instead, the company's highly popular two-cylinder tractors took over the role of being the company's most recognizable product.

Even though the company's most recognizable product had changed by 1935, most people still associated John Deere with only agricultural products. But that same year Deere & Company made big moves to expand its market base beyond the agricultural realm. During 1935, the company released its first tractors designated expressly for industrial applications: the Models AI and BI. And the move wasn't just a temporary one: John Deere meant business!

In the early days, Deere certainly had a few problems entering the industrial tractor market. But it seems likely that the fault didn't lie with Deere, but with the market itself. Deere made its move to enter the industrial tractor market when the nation was in the throes of the Great Depression. Thus, even though the company was producing industrial tractor models that were highly effective and quite versatile, the marketplace did not have the capital or the workload to take advantage of the offerings. Despite the weak sales, Deere & Company persevered and continued to work diligently on industrial tractor models and designs.

During and immediately after World War II, things really started coming together for Deere & Company in a variety of ways, including its industrial tractor production. The company's little Model LI had become very popular for such duties as roadside mowing, while another Deere tractor model—an agricultural model converted into a crawler—was seeing extensive use in forestry work.

With those two models in production, Deere had a strong foothold in the industrial tractor market, even though one of the models wasn't even a true industrial tractor. But Deere & Company realized the market potential of crawler tractors for a variety of industrial applications, including but not limited to forestry work. In 1949, Deere made a big move by producing its own all-Deere-built crawler tractor—the Model MC crawler. That same year, Deere also released the Model MI industrial tractor, a tractor very closely related to the MC. Furthermore, Deere did something else in 1949 that would have a strong impact on its future industrial tractors: it unveiled its first diesel tractor, the Model R. The company would quickly discover that the powerful R had much potential in industrial markets, as well.

Not long after their introduction, the Model M series tractors—including the MI and MC—were replaced by the 40 series tractors. The 40 would give way to the 420, which would in turn be supplanted by the 430. And then, Deere unveiled the Model 440, considered by many the first strictly industrial tractor in Deere's lineup. It wasn't an agricultural tractor that had been modified for industrial use like almost every other John Deere industrial tractor up to that point. The 440 had been designed specifically for industrial use, and it found itself useful and successful in a variety of ways.

Like the M series, the Model R tractors—tractors at the large end of the spectrum—soon found themselves being replaced by the Model 80, which in turn led to the Model 820, which soon thereafter gave way to the Model 830. Deere had by that time fully realized the industrial potential for this brawny series of tractors, and many of them had already seen industrial work. Some 820 tractors and specialized Model 830-I industrial tractors, for instance, were mated up with Hancock elevating scrapers and put to work building roads and doing other similar construction work. Those machines, though, would soon give way to the biggest thing (literally) to hit Deere's large industrial line to date—the Model 840.

Both the 440 and 840 did much to give Deere an even surer footing in the industrial market. Industrial customers of all sorts found the tractors highly successful, and Deere had by that time developed a marketing system that effectively promoted the industrial units. For years, Deere & Company had produced its agricultural and industrial units from common design origins. Thus Deere's industrials were basically just updated and specialized versions of agricultural tractor models. By the time Deere released the 440 and 840, however, the company had established its Industrial Division as a separate entity. After separating agricultural and industrial production, the company established factories and dealerships dedicated solely to industrial models. No longer were industrial John Deere tractors just yellow tractors with a few additions or renovations. They were now full-fledged industrials.

As successful as the 840 and 440 industrials were, Deere soon recognized that it had gaps in its industrial line that it wanted to fill. That's exactly what Deere & Company set out to do in the 1960s, and soon thereafter the company announced brand-new models that proved innovative, effective, and reliable. Before long, the lineup came to include (in part) motor graders, loaders, log loaders, log skidders, bulldozers, utility tractors, landscape loaders, backhoe loaders, skid steer loaders, forklifts, excavators, and so much more.

As the world and markets have changed, Deere & Company has changed along the way, too, in order to fit the needs of customers of the times. Often over the years, the company changed its logo in an attempt to reflect new design or market initiatives. This book addresses those changes, discussing how they relate to Deere's industrial tractor production. It seems no coincidence that most of Deere's logo changes have occurred when the company was making big advances in industrial markets.

Today, Deere produces a very long line of industrial machines. These products range from skid steer loaders to full-sized excavators, from backhoe loaders to forklifts, from feller bunchers to log loaders, and from small "Gator" utility vehicles to gargantuan articulated dump trucks. But that's just the beginning of Deere's industrial line.

John Deere industrial tractors can be found throughout the world and are very easy to spot working on a variety of construction projects across the land. Throughout time, John Deere industrials have been and continue to be wonderful machines. Furthermore, they have a wonderful history that deserves to be told. This book is an attempt to tell the stories of those machines.

How This Book Is Arranged

This book is largely arranged in chronological order. Sometimes the end of one chapter will overlap with the beginning of the next when a little foundation in the new chapter helps to clarify its subject matter. In a few spots, particularly in the last chapter, the arrangement becomes more topical. This approach works best for discrete subjects that are unique, or—as is the case in the last chapter—devoted to current John Deere industrials.

The Purpose of This Book

This book addresses John Deere industrial tractors from an enthusiast's standpoint. The information presented is for entertainment and basic educational purposes; in no way is this book intended to be a "buyer's guide" of sorts for people considering buying industrial tractors and machines. If you would like to learn more about John Deere industrial products—particularly those of today, but also those of the past—please visit your local John Deere dealer or sign on to their website at www.johndeere.com.

The author is not an employee or official representative of Deere & Company, and this book is not an official publication of that company.

CHAPTER 1

The Early John Deere Industrials

From the company's beginnings in 1837, John Deere produced farm implements for decades before entering tractor production. Once the company moved into the tractor business, it was quick to see and take advantage of industrial applications. Deere & Company was able to develop a successful tractor business quite swiftly, partly because of a sound business decision and in part due to good fortune.

When Deere first was considering entering the tractor market, the company looked at many different options. Deere tested a number of experimental tractor models, but none of these machines performed to the company's satisfaction. Instead of developing a tractor line from scratch or from prototype, Deere officials decided that a better course would be to purchase an established tractor manufacturer.

Deere & Company Enters the Tractor Market

The company that Deere ultimately purchased was the Waterloo Gasoline Engine Company of Waterloo, Iowa. That company, which had become renowned for its gasoline engines, had been producing tractors for several years at the time of the purchase, and numerous farmers knew the Waterloo Boy tractors to be reliable, effective units. Deere completed the transaction on March 14, 1918.

There were several advantages to purchasing an established company. In addition to acquiring a reputed line of tractors, Deere also benefited from a well-established dealer network, parts inventory, and more. At the time of the purchase, the Waterloo Gasoline Engine Company had two major Waterloo Boy models in production—the Models R and N. Furthermore, the company had some experimental models in development when Deere made the acquisition.

Waterloo had introduced the Waterloo Boy Model R four years before the Deere takeover, back in 1914. The R started production with a single-speed transmission and a two-cylinder 5.5x7-inch engine, but the company quickly made refinements. Waterloo's method for designating improved models was to add a second letter to the model name. With each

John Deere had been building tractors for only a few years when it introduced its first industrial versions. With the new yellow paint scheme, people who saw these machines at work must have known they were something special. *Andy Kraushaar*

Popular as an agricultural tractor particularly in grain-growing regions, the Model D John Deere became the foundation upon which Deere would build its first official industrial tractor. Although the DI didn't sell as well as Deere had hoped, later Deere industrials would prove exceptionally popular, thanks in part to descendants of the Model R, seen in the background.

new version, this letter advanced down the alphabet. By production's end in 1919, the model had used 13 such letters, ranging from A to M. The final version of the R, which was produced under Deere ownership, was designated Model RM. By that time, the model featured a 6.5x7-inch bore and stroke, but it still retained the single-speed transmission. The other Waterloo Boy model, the Model N, used a two-speed transmission and always used the 6.5x7-inch engine.

Along with the two tractor models and parts and distribution channels, Deere also acquired a good deal of experimental knowledge. Indeed, the Waterloo Gasoline Engine Company had been heavily engaged in experimentation on its Waterloo Boy tractors well before Deere came into the picture. The experimental Waterloo Boy models that were in the works looked drastically different from the company's regular production models. But they did look much like the popular tractor that

they would eventually evolve into—the two-cylinder John Deere Model D, which Deere would unleash in 1923.

The Model D was the first regular production two-cylinder tractor to bear the famous John Deere name. The D was a standard-tread tractor that used the same engine size as the Waterloo Boy Models RM and N, and it plowed with gusto. The D proved itself in agricultural realms quite well, making not only an effective plow tractor but also a tremendous performer

For most industrial jobs, steel wheels with lugs were not desirable. Looking for an effective alternative, Deere placed many of its early industrials on solid rubber tires. When pneumatic tires hit the scene in the late 1920s, Deere switched to that more pliable alternative on most of its industrial tractors. This Model D features both front and rear pneumatic rubber tires. *Randy Leffingwell*

on the belt. The Waterloo Boy Models N and R had been great tractors, too, but the D set a new standard of agricultural excellence for Deere & Company. The D became the basis for Deere's most noticeable early attempts to venture into the industrial tractor market.

The Early Industrialized Model Ds

As good a tractor as the D was, it wasn't perfectly suited to industrial applications. It could pull a road grader, but not on asphalt or

concrete surfaces because the D's steel wheels damaged them—rubber tires weren't yet an option on the D. In addition, industrial applications often required different operating speeds. To better serve potential industrial customers, Deere decided to make changes that would result in a more specialized Model D.

By 1925, Deere & Company produced a handful of Model Ds outfitted with special equipment to satisfy certain industrial needs. To address the problem of the D's steel

wheels damaging concrete and similar surfaces, Deere outfitted many of these special tractors with solid rubber tires. Deere also installed special 28-tooth sprockets in these tractors' rear ends to help them better meet the speed needs of industrial applications. Powering these industrialized Ds was the same engine used on the original agricultural models—the 465-ci horizontal two-cylinder powerplant with its 6.5-inch bore and 7-inch stroke.

Eventually, these industrialized Model Ds came to be known as the

One of the most fascinating early John Deere industrial derivatives, the John Deere Model D Hawkeye Motor Patrol, has captured the interest of many in today's collector world. These machines appear to have been relatively successful at the jobs they were designed to do, despite the fact that only a handful of the units ever saw production. Unfortunately, none are known to exist today. *Deere & Company Archives*

"John Deere Industrial Tractors." Deere used that terminology in its 1926 advertising literature for the model. According to that literature, the "John Deere Industrial Tractor" came fitted with 40x8-inch rear wheels and 24x3 1/2-inch front wheels with hard, plain rubber tires. The D's typical 38-tooth sprockets could be replaced by either 28- or 22-tooth sprockets, both of which afforded a higher gear ratio. The 28-tooth sprockets gave the tractor a road speed of 4 miles per hour and

a low speed of 3 miles per hour. The 22-tooth sprockets, which had to be used in conjunction with 50-inch rear wheels, provided even faster speeds—5 miles per hour in road gear, and 3 3/4 miles per hour in low. Options for this model included wheel weight sets weighing 400, 500, 1,800, or 1,900 pounds per pair. Yet another option for this model was a 40x5-inch extension wheel with rubber tire. Deere was well on its way to establishing itself in the industrial tractor market.

Deere Expands the Industrial D's Uses

The industrial economy was expanding and new manufacturers and new products were entering the market. Deere management decided that it could increase sales by coupling its tractor with quality industrial implements produced by other companies. With this collaborative strategy, Deere could expand its tractor's utility without taking on the manufacturing and development costs for the implements.

Deere had designed the basic Model D tractor as a stout unit with a number of brawny components. The company learned from the early Model Ds that even agricultural tractors endured many jolts and jars — especially when going over uneven ground or coming out of, going into, or driving across furrows. Thus, Deere made sure that the later Ds featured a heavy-duty front axle. That front axle was heavy enough that it could withstand almost any load or challenge it might endure in industrial applications as well. *Andy Kraushaar*

Perhaps the most interesting attachment that Deere authorized for its industrial Model Ds was a road grader (otherwise known as a road maintainer). In order to convert its Model D into a road grader, Deere & Company worked with the Hawkeye Maintainer Company from Waterloo, Iowa. That company's Hawkeye Motor Patrol road grader was attached to specialized versions of the Model D. The result became known as the John Deere Model D Hawkeye Motor Patrols; they were the first road grader versions of John Deere tractors.

Most of the Model D Hawkeye Motor Patrol tractors left Deere fitted with special rubber-tired rear wheels. The majority of those Ds came fitted with dual rear wheels, an option not often seen on even the industrial versions of the D. Deere also fitted these special D tractors with a larger-capacity fuel tank, different brake parts, and a different platform that didn't feature the traditional fenders normally found on Model D tractors.

The Hawkeye Motor Patrol road maintainer unit looks quite different from the typical road graders of today. In addition to the obvious difference in the power supply for the unit—using the D's two-cylinder engine instead of being drawn by horses or powered by a tractor with a four-cylinder engine—the actual grader attachment itself was more sophisticated

Start it by hand! And, no, that's not an option — at least it wasn't throughout most of the Model DI's production. To start these tractors, one first needed to make sure the tractor was out of gear, the gas was turned on, and the compression-relief valves (also known as "petcocks") on the engine were open. Then, the person would roll over the big flywheel on the left side of the tractor's engine until the powerplant barked to life. *Randy Leffingwell*

than the traditional pull-type road maintainers of the era. Whereas the pull-type graders usually required two operators if tractor-drawn, the Hawkeye could be operated easily by the driver of the tractor. The grader appears to have used both a worm drive-type system and a more basic bolt-adjustment system for changing the position of the blade. Thus, the grader's blade position could not be altered in all necessary ways from the operator's station on the tractor. For its time, however, the D Hawkeye Motor Patrol did have a very sophisticated system and did do its job well. It was a steppingstone in the right direction.

Production of the D Hawkeye Motor Patrols lasted through only

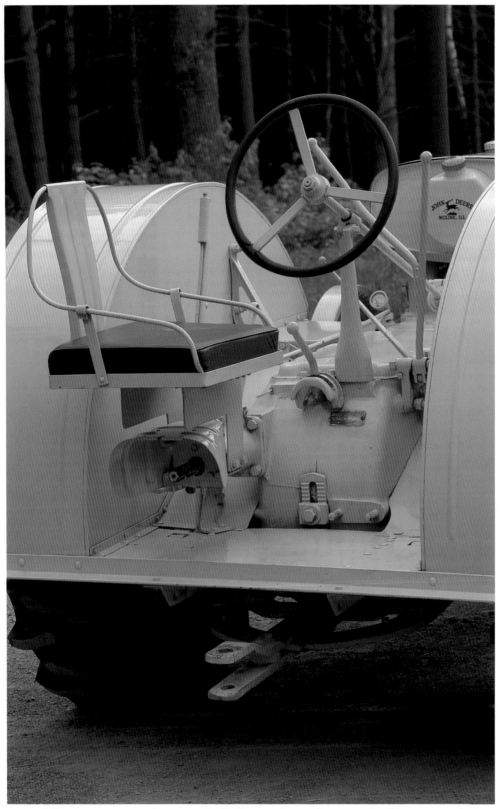

This Model DI features a special seat, mounted sideways, that made it easier for the operator to both control and keep tabs on drawn equipment while still maintaining control of the tractor. Another special feature on this DI is the power takeoff, which provided yet another way to supply power to drawn equipment. *Randy Leffingwell*

about three model years, from 1929 to 1931. Not many John Deere Ds in that period received the road grader conversion. Deere & Company would soon abandon the road grader market, only to return in the 1960s when it would set the standard for road graders in the decades to come.

A Year of Changes: 1935

By 1935, Deere had expanded its agricultural tractor production tremendously. In addition to the stalwart standard-tread Model D, Deere also had two row-crop tractor models in production, the Model A (a direct-line descendant of Deere's earlier row-crop tractor, the GP) and the Model B. In 1935, Deere & Company further diversified its tractor lineup by introducing specialized versions of the A and B series tractors. These versions included single-front-wheel and wide-adjustable front-axle versions of the basic models, plus even more striking derivatives—Deere even released standard-tread versions of the two models, including both regular agricultural models and orchard versions.

Although the company made no new additions to its industrial tractor line in 1935, it did have new models in development. Equally important, 1935 was the year the company made a significant change to model designations. During that year, the company decided to give its specialized tractor versions letter designations to reflect each model's particular purpose.

The D Industrial Becomes the Model DI

Under the new naming system, the single-front-wheeled version of the A and B became known as the Models AN and BN—the "N" indicating that the tractors had a "Narrow" front end, which meant that they had a single front wheel. Likewise, the wide-adjustable front-axle versions of the A and B became known as the AW and BW, "W" meaning "Wide." Deere designated the basic standard-tread versions of the A and B as Models AR and BR, the "R" meaning "Regular" or fixed rear tread widths. The orchard versions of those models received the designations AO and BO. The company's industrial models were not left out of the new system. Thus, late in 1935, Deere renamed the Model D industrial versions Model DI.

The Official Color of Industrials: Yellow

Deere & Company was getting very serious about its venture into the industrial tractor market, and the company realized that it would probably be best to distinguish its industrial tractors as much as possible from its agricultural units. In addition to giving the industrials their own separate designations, Deere also decided to paint the industrial tractors in colors distinct from their agricultural models—a trend that continues to this day. In Deere's Branch House Bulletin No. 781 of July 16, 1935, Frank Silloway wrote, "To further differentiate the agricultural tractors from the industrial

tractors, industrial tractors will be painted <u>Hi-Way</u> Yellow." The industrial tractors would also receive black stenciling, yet another feature that has stood the test of time on Deere industrials. Silloway also noted that Deere's agricultural dealers would not be allowed to distribute the company's industrial tractors, and vice versa. In January 1936, Deere's R.B. Lourie wrote in Branch House Bulletin No. 798, "It is becoming increasingly evident that we should completely segregate the industrial side of our business from the agricultural side." And it is clear that Deere was trying to do just that.

The DI Gets Tires

By the time the DI became an official model in the Deere lineup, pneumatic rubber tires had been increasing in popularity for several years. Inflatable rubber tires started appearing on tractors in the late 1920s, but they were initially a novel option that only a handful of farmers chose to add to their agricultural tractors. Word quickly got out, though, that rubber tires were indeed superior to steel wheels for a number of reasons. For one, the rubber tires typically provided better flotation, not compacting the soil as much as steel wheels did.

Another thing that rubber tires proved to be was versatile. Wheel designers struggled for years to manufacture steel wheels that would be suitable for a wide variety of soil conditions, but no single steel wheel type did well. For

instance, tiptoe steel wheels provided great traction in most soils, but their narrowness caused them to cut too deeply into soft ground. Wide-faced steel wheels with attached lugs couldn't be used for all farming applications either, proving perhaps least satisfactory in row-crop cultivation. For those applications, narrower wheels were necessary. Yet another problem with steel wheels was that their lugs tended to tear up the surfaces they passed over, whether pastures, dirt roads, or paved roads, the latter of which were beginning to appear at that time. Rubber tires, by contrast, worked well in many soil conditions, did little or no damage to driving surfaces, and even provided the farmer with a more comfortable ride. In addition, because they absorbed shock and rolled more smoothly, rubber tires allowed farmers to drive their tractors faster, whether plowing a field or hauling a cart to market.

Because of their many advantages and increasing popularity, Deere decided to make low-pressure pneumatic tires standard on its Model DI. These tires replaced the solid rubber tires the company typically fitted to the tractor's steel wheels for industrial applications. Other items that Deere made standard on the DI included the 28-tooth sprockets in the rear end, an extension for the brake control lever, and an extension for the swinging drawbar. Buyers of the Model DI got all of those things for a base price of only $1,556.50.

Options for Industrials: Another Key to Success

As good as the standard-equipment features of the Model DI were, those things weren't all that a buyer could get in a Model DI. Deere knew that special customers had special needs, and the company tried to satisfy as many of those needs as it could by making many items optional on the Model DI. For instance, Deere offered the basic Model DI with the addition of a power takeoff (PTO) and the related control assembly for a total of only $1,713.00. A buyer wanting to order a DI with special wheel equipment could do so and still be able to get the PTO if desired. In that case, the entire PTO assembly cost only $156.50 extra. Other things Deere made optional on the DI starting with the 1936 model year included a pair of rear wheel weights (300 pounds total) for $17.00, a high-speed sprocket assembly for only $10.00, and "direct generator lighting equipment" for $71.50. Deere also made hand-operated rear-wheel brakes available for the Model DI as an option by February of 1936.

Buyers could also purchase special versions of the DI that featured, in part, different wheel sizes—sometimes requiring the rear platform, fenders, and seat to be left off the tractor. The special wheel packages included 40x8 high-pressure rear tires (either singles or duals), 42x9 high-pressure rear tires (either singles or duals), 32x6 front tires, 28x6 front steel wheels, and 46x12 rear steel

wheels. Customers could also order 6- or 12-inch extension steel rims to go along with the 46x12 rear steel wheels. Obviously, Deere & Company made the DI available in a wide array of configurations that could suit many different needs. By the spring of 1936, Deere had also approved and started installing low-pressure dual rear tires on the Model DI.

Yet another Deere industrial product resulted from the Model D. It wasn't a tractor, though—it was a power unit. The Type W power units were basically converted Model D engines on skids (standard), which Deere classified as "Industrial Power Units." One interesting conversion kit that Deere offered for the Type W engines was an attachment to convert the unit to natural gas instead of the standard kerosene or other low-grade fuels on which the engines were typically run.

Deere Reveals an Expanded Industrial Line: The 1936 National Road Show

Starting in March 1936, Deere released two new industrial tractor models that it had been developing behind the scenes. Derivatives of the standard-tread versions of the Models A and B, these tractors were known as the Models AI and BI. The company was excited about the possibilities for these models. In Deere's Branch House Bulletin No. 791 of November 22, 1935, R.B. Lourie stated: "It is our confident belief that these two new industrial models, namely, the AI and the BI, will open up a much

broader field for industrial tractor business than the DI model."

Two New Tractors Revealed: The Models AI and BI

Even though the AI and BI weren't officially offered at the beginning of 1936, pre-production versions of both models were apparently displayed in January of that year. According to Deere documents, Deere participated in the National Road Show at Cleveland, Ohio, from January 20 to 24, 1936. The following week, Deere's Branch House Bulletin No. 798 of January 31, 1936, states, "We made our initial bow to the public with our industrial tractors, power unit and industrial tractor mower by exhibiting these products at the National Road show . . . We may have been premature in making this exhibit, because we are not yet in production of the AI and BI tractors in quantities, but we felt that this showing was necessary because such shows are only held every two or three years."

The Caterpillar Connection: A Marketing Proposal

The Bulletin just mentioned also helps explain one of the ways in which Deere tried to get started in the industrial business. Deere's exhibit sat right next to that of the Caterpillar Tractor Company, which at the time was well known in the industrial realm, particularly for its crawler tractors. At the time, however, Caterpillar had not entered the wheel tractor market, so Deere decided to make Caterpillar a

Thanks to the new Model AI, the DI John Deere was no longer alone in the company's industrial tractor lineup. The AI shared many features with the larger Model DI, but the new model's more compact size made it a better performer for some industrial jobs. *Randy Leffingwell*

proposition: Deere offered Caterpillar the sole rights to distribute Deere's industrial tractors and equipment, and Caterpillar accepted the proposal by late 1935. Accordingly, Deere published its Branch House Bulletin No. 792 on November 30 of that year, stating, "It is the policy of Deere & Company to market its industrial tractors and equipment through Caterpillar Tractor Co. industrial distributors."

But just because Caterpillar itself agreed to the proposition didn't mean that Caterpillar's distributors themselves had to participate. Consequently, Deere approached the Caterpillar distributors who were present at the 1936 National Road Show, and most of them were quite interested in Deere's proposal. Those same Caterpillar distributors also confirmed Deere's belief that it would be best if Deere established a

The Model AI, the second official industrial tractor in Deere's line, was soon joined by the smaller Model BI industrial tractor. These two smaller models, like the DI that came before them, ordinarily received a yellow paint job with black lettering. *Andy Kraushaar*

Based upon the standard-tread Model BR tractor, the Model BI was more than just cute. A reliable, stout tractor, it shared many characteristics with the BR, but the industrial was slightly more maneuverable, thanks to a shorter wheelbase. *Andy Kraushaar*

The Model AI John Deere was the company's first tractor that could be fitted with a special crane attachment. The LaPlant-Choate crane made the AI into something that no John Deere tractor had ever been before. Interestingly, though, despite the success the AI enjoyed with many other such attachments, Deere did not specifically make the AI available as the powerplant for a road maintainer, as had been the case with the industrial Model D tractors. *Andy Kraushaar*

These heavy rear-wheel weights did more than just give the AI a firm grip on the situation. They also served as a counterbalance for the heavy loads this machine could lift with the crane attachment. Note that this tractor also features hard rubber tires on the front end. *Andy Kraushaar*

line of auxiliary equipment designed specifically to work with its line of industrial tractors. As a result, Deere quickly made moves to achieve those goals by contacting suppliers of such equipment to see what arrangements could be made.

Other Industrial Equipment Shown

Among the other products that Deere presented at the 1936 National Road Show was its line of industrial tractor mowers. Deere had designed those mowers specifically for use with its DI, AI, and BI tractors, and they were all of the foot-lift type. Deere offered these mowers with 6-foot and 7-foot cutter bars for all three tractor models. Deere also made hand-lift derivatives of those same mowers available for Caterpillar's Model No. 22, 28, and 40 crawler tractors.

The Model AI Begins Production

Production of the Model AI tractors officially began in mid-March 1936, roughly two months after the National Road Show in Cleveland. Deere & Company's Engineering Decision D6100 of February 15, 1936, announced the new model, but the company didn't officially initiate production of the AI until just over one month after that date. Then, about one month after that, the first complete Model AI tractor—serial number 252334—rolled off the line in late April 1936.

The new Model AI tractor had much to offer to the industrial world. Based on the standard-tread

Model AR John Deere tractor, the AI shared many characteristics with its agricultural counterpart. For instance, both models featured the 309-ci engine that was also used in the basic row-crop Model A John Deere tractors. That engine produced around 24 brake horsepower when burning distillate fuel. Similarly, the AI used a four-speed transmission, used a standard-tread chassis, and weighed in at around 3,800 pounds. But the AI wasn't exactly like the AR. For one thing, the AI had a somewhat shorter turning radius. This was made possible by relocating the AI's front axle 7 inches back from where it had been located on the AR. Thus, instead of a 76-inch wheelbase, the AI now had a 69-inch wheelbase. Deere knew that industrial tractors often worked in closer quarters than did agricultural models operating in the fields.

Relocating the front axle also facilitated the use of front-mounted attachments. For balance, Deere wanted such attachments to be located as close to the radiator as possible. Moving the front axle back allowed the attachments to come back as well. To further facilitate front-mounted attachments, the AI's front axle also featured special finished pads and tapped accessory-mounting holes.

Model BI Production Begins

Deere & Company officially started regular production of the new Model BI later in the month of March 1936. The company announced the start of production

Yellow wasn't always the only color one could get on a Deere industrial tractor. Some municipal and even state governments deemed yellow not noticeable enough for most industrial activities, so Deere had to offer other colors to meet those customers' needs. The red on this Model BI is just one of many different colors that Deere's industrial tractors have worn over time. *Andy Kraushaar*

with its Engineering Decision D6150, which came just three days after the decision announcing the Model AI's commencement of production. Decision D6150 pointed out that the Model BI—which Deere had derived from the basic Model BR tractor—had had its front axle scooted back 5 1/4 inches from its original position. That change gave the BI two more advantages for use in industrial applications when compared to the Models BR and BO. These advantages were the same as those gained by the AI—namely, a shorter turning radius and the opportunity to mount attachments closer to the tractor's radiator for improved balance and reduced front-end stress. Like the AI, the BI was much like its agricultural counterpart. The BI featured the same basic engine as used in the BR—a traditional two-cylinder horizontal engine with a 4.25x5.25-inch bore and stroke—and the same four-speed transmission.

Special Equipment Approved for Use on AI and BI

To maximize the AI and BI models' market potential, Deere quickly began approving allied, or related, equipment for use on the models. By June 1936, Deere & Company had approved the use of two different models of Willamette-Hyster Company hoists on the Model AI. The two approved models included the Model JD-AS single-drum Hyster and the Model JD-AD double-drum Hyster.

The engine side covers on this 1936 Model AI tractor provided extra protection for the tractor's engine, but may have had other advantages, depending on the unit's working environment. For instance, this tractor — especially with its orchard-style air intake caps — has few obstructions to block the operator's view and is also less likely to get caught up on anything it might be working around. *Randy Leffingwell*

The optional cab on this Model AI gave the operator a more comfortable, safer workstation. This cab also shows Deere's early dedication to providing cabs with excellent visibility for the operator, a dedication that persists to this day. *Randy Leffingwell*

Both cranes made use of a special optional side power shaft that Deere made by converting the Model AI's first reduction gear cover.

In the fall of 1937, Deere approved the use of a crane attachment on the Model AI. That crane—the Model CA crane manufactured by the LaPlant-Choate Manufacturing Company, Inc., of Cedar Rapids, Iowa—operated off the AI's side power shaft and was the first of its kind on a John Deere tractor. The CA crane could handle loads between 2,700 and 3,400 pounds when its boom was fully retracted (the handling capacities of the crane varied depending on the types of wheel equipment used on the underlying Model AI). If the crane's boom was fully extended, however, the handling capacity fell to between 1,700 and 2,300 pounds.

In 1938, Deere approved the use of its own street flusher and sprinkler with the AI. Then, two years later, Deere approved the use of two snowplows with the AI, manufactured by the Wm. Bros. Boiler and Manufacturing Co. of Minneapolis, Minnesota. These plows—the "SNO-FLYR" Models EH and EHW—had to be used with AIs fitted with 6.5x16-inch six-ply front tires.

Obviously, Deere & Company had already made some big moves in fulfilling the needs of industrial customers with tractors by 1937. At that time, Deere had three industrial tractor models in regular production, and their sizes covered a fairly broad range.

DID YOU KNOW?
EARLY LINDEMAN CRAWLERS

After becoming a John Deere dealer early in the twentieth century, the Lindeman Power Equipment Company of Yakima, Washington, began converting John Deere tractors to crawlers in the early 1930s. Lindeman first converted at least one Model D (and possibly even a few more) into crawlers using tracks from a Best crawler. But the D John Deere Lindeman crawler handled similarly to the way that the standard-tread wheatland-type Model D wheel tractors handled—without superb maneuverability. Lindeman quickly figured out that the model wasn't ideal for use in the orchards around Yakima, but it could be used with some success for more basic agricultural applications, such as plowing fields. Still, though, the regular Model D agricultural models did those jobs just fine without modifications.

Even though the John Deere D Lindeman project didn't pan out, the Lindeman company didn't stop trying to put Deere tractors on tracks. Instead, it shifted its focus to the Model GPO John Deere tractors. The GPO already had many features that made it appealing to orchard growers, including a lowered operator position and a low-clearance exhaust and air intake. Lindeman made the conversions necessary to add the track system, and the result was fairly impressive. A number of the roughly two-dozen GPO Lindeman crawlers featured fenders that helped keep tree limbs out of the track assemblies. Some of those fenders were little more than sheet steel that extended over the top of the crawler tracks, whereas others were true orchard and grove-type fenders covering not only the tops of the tracks but also extending down the outside of the track assemblies.

The GPO John Deere Lindeman crawlers were fairly successful, but some people still felt that the GPO crawlers were a bit too large for orchard use. And like the D crawlers, some of the GPO Lindemans found themselves out in the open air plowing fields and doing other non-orchard work. For those who thought the GPO crawlers too large or not nimble enough, things were about to change. Deere discontinued production of the GPO and the rest of the GP series in 1935, but it didn't forget about its orchard and grove customers. The GPO was soon to be replaced by the Model AO and an even smaller model, the Model BO. The AO never received track assemblies, but it was only a matter of time before many of the Model B standard-tread tractors (the Model BO tractors in particular) found themselves atop tracks courtesy the Lindeman Power Equipment Company.

The John Deere GPO Lindeman-converted crawler became the second John Deere on tracks. This unit, somewhat popular for orchard work, also proved usable in some more traditional farm jobs. This model is one of the oldest ancestors to Deere's current popular bulldozer line. *Randy Leffingwell*

When Lindeman converted Deere's tractors into crawlers, the company had to add steering brakes and related controls to the units in addition to the track assemblies. Lindeman did such a good job of making John Deeres into crawlers that Deere & Company eventually bought out the Yakima, Washington-based company. *Randy Leffingwell*

Interestingly, this 1935 model John Deere GPO Lindeman crawler doesn't have support rollers for its track assemblies. Some of these crawlers did feature one centrally located support roller for each track, however. Support rollers or not, these tractors helped set the stage for future Deere crawler success. *Randy Leffingwell*

DEERE TRADEMARK LOGO CORNER: CHANGES IN 1936 AND 1937

Over the years, Deere & Company has decided to change its logo several times, and such changes typically occur whenever the company itself is undergoing—or has recently undergone—noticeable changes. The fact that Deere changed its trademark logo twice in the 1930s could be considered a good barometer for the amount of change the company was undergoing at the time.

Deere made the first of these revisions in 1936. That trademark logo had a unique design for Deere, immediately recognizable by its border alone. The border featured six points, three on the top half and three on the bottom half, and was the first border ever used as part of the Deere & Company trademark logo. The logo retained the famous figure of a deer jumping over a log with the words "JOHN" and "DEERE" to the left and right of the deer's head, but in this version the deer and log were solid silhouettes instead of detailed renditions. Below the deer appeared the words "MOLINE, ILL." and below that were the words "THE TRADE MARK OF QUALITY MADE FAMOUS BY GOOD IMPLEMENTS".

Deere's new logo for 1936 didn't stay around for long. The company replaced it the very next year. The 1937 trademark logo was much simpler, lacking both the unique border and the signature phrase. The absence of the phrase in the 1937 trademark logo tells us much about the company's changing focus.

When Deere started using the words "THE TRADE MARK OF QUALITY MADE FAMOUS BY GOOD IMPLEMENTS" in its 1912 logo, they definitely rang true. At the time, Deere & Company's primary products were its implements, and Deere certainly made an understatement by describing them simply as "good." By the mid-1930s, however, Deere & Company had clearly established itself as a producer of quality farm machinery, but its product list had grown tremendously since 1912. The most important new farm machinery Deere produced by the mid-1930s were its tractors. And, like its famous implements, Deere's tractors were certainly high-quality units. So it made sense that Deere would choose to broaden its image by removing any reference to implements from its trademark logo. The 1937 change seems to clearly reflect the company's success with agricultural tractors, but it likely also gives some hint of the company's efforts in the industrial tractor market as well.

The Model BI served as Deere's smallest industrial tractor, while the Model DI was its biggest. The mid-sized Model AI was perhaps the most versatile of the three models, however, and its size was "just right" for many applications. But even with three respectable industrial tractors in production, Deere wanted to do more in this market sector.

Yellow Isn't the Only Industrial Color

In the summer of 1937, Deere made an interesting (and certainly colorful) decision to help satisfy the needs of its industrial customers. Prior to that time, most of Deere's industrial tractor models had been painted yellow with black lettering. Deere had made that practice official back in late 1935 when the company formally introduced the Model DI. But Deere realized that certain industrial customers preferred to buy industrial tractors painted some color other than highway yellow; still other customers were required by state, local, or city laws to paint their industrial tractors some specific color that wasn't highway yellow. Thus, in the summer of 1937, Deere & Company made additional special paint colors available for all of its industrial tractors. Those colors included light red, gray, blue, orange, green (different from the standard John Deere green, which customers could also specify for industrial tractors), and yellows other than highway yellow.

If Deere was counting on new color options increasing sales, those expectations went virtually unmet initially. No one knows for certain how many Model AI, BI, and DI tractors received those special paint colors, but it would seem that very few did. Indeed, it's entirely possible that no Model AI or DI received special paint. Apparently, the factory did paint at least one Model BI red to fill a special order, though, and this tractor still exists to this day.

One reason more customers didn't take advantage of the special colors is that they didn't need to. The laws requiring particular colors for certain equipment typically applied to machines used on or near roads, such as mowers and street sweepers. Since the models AI, BI, and DI weren't typically handling those jobs, customers had no incentive to special order a particular color. Deere & Company may simply have been covering its bases, though, by approving the use of special colors on its industrial tractors, for the company would soon introduce a small tractor that would take advantage of that option.

Lovable Littler Letter Series Industrials Introduced

The story of the Model 62 and its descendants began back in the mid-1930s when Deere recognized the needs of many small farmers for a tractor that was smaller and less expensive than the John Deere B. Responding, the company ordered its engineers at the John Deere Wagon Works in Moline, Illinois, to begin working on a new tractor design. The first tangible results appeared with the experimental Model Y of 1936. The Y soon evolved into the John Deere Model 62 tractor, which Deere began producing on a limited basis early in 1937 (prior to announcing the approval of additional colors for industrial tractors). The Model 62 had a very short production life, ending production by late 1937. But then the Model 62 evolved into yet another new model: the Model L.

Like the 62, the new Model L was envisioned primarily as an agricultural tractor. But Deere did make an industrial derivative of the Model L available almost from the start of its production beginning in the 1938 model year. It is important to note that, like the first industrial versions of the Model D, these early Model Ls were not yet officially designated Model LIs. The industrial L differed very little from the regular, original agricultural version of the model—the main difference between the two versions being the colors they were painted.

Initially, the industrial versions of the Model L didn't seem to take much (if any) advantage of the new special colors that Deere had approved. Instead, like most Deere industrial tractors, the industrial Ls were painted some shade of yellow. It is possible that a few Model Ls produced during the 1938 model year (the only year during which the L was "unstyled," see Styling Issues, following) received special paint colors, but records for those units no longer exist. However, Deere's Serial Number Registers do still exist for the styled Model L tractors, which Deere introduced in the 1939 model year. In a number of instances, those records indicate when styled Model Ls were painted any color other than the standard John Deere green (which, of course, was the main body color for the agricultural Model Ls). Thus, by looking at those records, one can determine fairly easily which styled Ls could be considered industrial versions. Model L serial number 625073—just 74 tractors into styled Model L production—is the first styled L noted as being painted a specific color; it was painted simply "yellow." The next tractor with a specifically identified paint color is serial number 625075; its color was the official color for the majority of Deere's industrial tractors at the time—highway yellow. Deere's Serial Number Registers seem to indicate that yellow and highway yellow were the only special colors used on the 1939 and early 1940 model styled L tractors. No evidence exists that the L up to that point had used any additional special colors, but that was about to change. The industrial versions of the L proved themselves very popular for performing roadside duties, and it was only a matter of time before someone would want one of those tractors but either need or want it painted some color other than yellow or John Deere green.

Changing Times: Styling Issues

By 1939, Deere & Company had clearly exhibited the fact that it wanted to consider its industrial tractor production as being separate from its regular agricultural production. And, in many ways, the company treated those models differently than it treated their agricultural counterparts. For instance, it seemed that Deere didn't mind having its industrial tractors remain in unstyled form, even after the company made big moves to stylize its most popular agricultural models at the start of and during the 1939 model year, including the row-crop versions of the Models A and B. Then, not long after 1939 model production began, Deere stylized its popular standard-tread Model D. While those agricultural models were stylized, though, the industrial Models AI, BI, and even the DI remained unstyled.

So, starting in 1939, most of Deere's industrial tractors remained in unstyled form for whatever reason. But the industrial versions of the Model L seemed to go against the grain of Deere industrial production. For instance, the industrial Ls didn't remain in unstyled form after the agricultural versions of that model were styled in 1939; they were styled right along with the agricultural versions (making them the first and only styled industrial tractors in Deere's line for several years). Additionally, even though by 1939 Deere had designated its industrial versions of the Models D, A, and B with a special model designation—the basic model series designation followed by an "I"—the industrial versions of the L still didn't adhere to that system of model designation. They still weren't officially Model LI tractors yet; instead, they continued to be classified merely as industrial versions of the Model L.

While the 1939 stylizations of many of Deere's agricultural models took the headlines that year, Deere's industrial tractor production didn't make the headlines in any noticeable fashion. The following model year would be similar. After all, Deere introduced a wide array of improvements for its 1940 model agricultural tractors, but the industrial tractors didn't appear to receive much attention. But 1940 was far more important for Deere's industrial tractor production than one might imagine, and it was all because of just one single tractor.

An Industrial on Tracks

In 1940, one single Model BI tractor—serial number 330986—was changed in a way that no Deere industrial tractor had ever been changed before. And it wasn't even Deere that made the modifications. The Lindeman Power Equipment Company of Yakima, Washington, took a 1940 Model BI and fitted tracks to it. This machine changed the company product line forever, marking the beginning of the Deere industrial crawler tractor.

Lindeman's conversion proved that the standard-tread B series John Deere tractors worked well when converted to crawler tractors. Despite that fact, Lindeman didn't convert another standard-tread Model B series tractor into a crawler for quite some time. Starting in early 1941, Deere's production of the standard-tread B tractors as a whole—including the Model BI—slowed to a crawl. The company manufactured fewer than 400 standard-tread Bs in 1941, and production remained at or near that same level through the 1944 model year.

Models AI, BI, and DI Discontinued

The problems for Deere's industrial tractor production weren't just limited to the low production figures of the BI, however. Indeed, on the surface, things had started looking pretty dismal for almost all of Deere's industrial tractor production by 1941. Sales of the Models AI, BI, and DI were far from impressive; indeed, in six years of production, Deere had produced and sold fewer than 500 of all of its industrial tractor models combined. By the summer of 1941, Deere & Company decided to drop the Models AI, BI, and DI from production. That decision appeared in both the company's Branch House Bulletin 918 of May 17, 1941, and its Engineering Decision D9900 of June 12, 1941. Branch House Bulletin No. 918 also stated that Deere & Company would "no longer be in position to supply bumper plates, special hitches, special brakes, special speeds, etc." on those tractors for use in industrial applications. Thus, at first glance, it may seem as if the era of John Deere industrial production was coming to a close in 1941; but, as most people know, looks are sometimes very deceiving.

Even though the first B series tractor placed on tracks was an industrial, it was also the last Model BI put on tracks. By the time Lindeman resumed its practice of putting the standard-tread B tractors on track assemblies, Deere & Company had dropped the Model BI. As a result, Lindeman switched to the BO and BR models, the BOs being the most popular model for that purpose. *Randy Leffingwell*

CHAPTER 2

John Deere Industrials During the War Years

John Deere had certainly firmly established itself as a top producer of farm tractors by the late 1930s. By that time, the company had also been trying for several years to get a similar firm footing in the industrial tractor industry. The company hadn't found much success in that market, though; in fact, sales of the AI, BI, and DI industrial tractors had been far from promising, leading Deere management to eliminate those models from the company's lineup. Deere & Company produced its last Model DI in early March of 1941, and the last AI in mid-June of that year. The last BI rolled off the lines at about the same time. According to Engineering Decision D9900, the three models were officially taken off Deere's books on July 1, 1941. But John Deere industrial production wasn't down for the count. During the first half of the 1940s, the company did much to solidify itself as a producer of industrial tractors.

Despite the fact that regular production of the AI, BI, and DI was coming to a close, both Branch House Bulletin No. 918 and Engineering Decision D9900 indicate that special paint colors were still going to be available on regular agricultural tractors that buyers intended to use for nonagricultural applications. The same held true for the Model L, which Deere still made available in an industrial version, even though it didn't yet have the official industrial tractor model designation of Model LI.

Starting in late 1940, the industrial versions of the styled L started using more specialized colors. Deere's Serial Number Registers indicate that late 1940 model Ls serial numbered 633035 to 633039 were painted "burnt orange." The list of special colors used on the industrial styled Ls then grew greatly in the 1941 model year. For instance, the Serial Number Registers show that tractors 633341, 633344, 633348, and 633358 through 633360 were all painted a "special yellow." Then, shades of orange became the predominant color used on those tractors, as tractor 633361 was painted a "special orange," and tractors 633362, 633363, and 633370 through 633376 were all painted "Tenn. orange" (which likely means "Tennessee orange"). The Serial Number

Despite Deere's limited success in its early efforts to establish itself as an industrial tractor manufacturer, two small tractors laid a foundation for future success: One was a true industrial tractor, the little Model LI. The other was not even really an industrial officially, but it took on a number of industrial-related roles in its active lifespan. That model was the Model BO Lindeman, seen here. *Randy Leffingwell*

The John Deere Model LI: an industrial tractor with style! Even though Deere did produce a few unstyled Model L tractors for industrial use, the actual Model LI always had styled lines. It was the beginning of a styling revolution that would change the face of Deere industrial machines forever. *Andy Kraushaar*

Registers also show that one 1941 Model L, serial number 633364, was painted a "special color," though no known documents describe it.

Another L with Industrial Aspirations: The Model LA

Whenever things started looking dim for Deere's industrial tractor production prospects, the L series tractors always seemed to somehow lighten things up. Starting in late 1940, the series gave yet another boost to Deere's industrial tractor production. At that time, Deere & Company introduced an enhanced version of its Model L, the Model LA.

The Model LA had several features not available on the original model that made it all the more appealing to industrial customers and farmers. First of all, the LA featured a larger engine; its 1/4-inch bigger bore gave the model an additional 11 inches of displacement. Deere also increased the engine's rated rpm by 300. Those changes caused a boost of about 4 horsepower on both the belt and the drawbar. The LA also weighed more than the L, a feature that helped deliver that additional horsepower to the ground more effectively. Deere gave the LA its additional weight in part by building the model with a heavy round bar stock frame, as opposed to the L's tubelike frame. Deere & Company also boosted the LA's front-end clearance, making standard the extended front spindles that had been available as an option on the basic Model L. Because of all these improvements, the LA attracted the attention of a number of industrial customers.

Some evidence suggests that the company did make the model available with industrial features and paint job, though these derivatives were not called LAI models—just as the company hadn't called the industrial derivatives of the Model L the Model LI . . . at least not yet.

The LI and the War Years

In May of 1941, just as it was closing down the AI, BI and DI models, Deere & Company shifted the industrial production mantle to the Model L, renaming it the Model LI. With the name change, the company assigned an all-new serial number run to the model. This was the first time a Deere industrial tractor received its own run of serial numbers. Along with the change in name and the new serial number run, the industrial version of the L also experienced a few design changes. For one, the tractor featured a larger-capacity fuel tank, a strengthened front axle

What happened to all that tall grass on the roadsides? The John Deere Model LI with side-mounted sickle mower conquered it. Even though Deere's industrial tractors clear back to the industrial Model Ds had been available with mowers, the Model LI proved the first astounding success in that capacity for Deere. Today, yellow John Deere tractors appear along roadsides throughout the nation. *Andy Kraushaar*

with shorter spindles, and a higher-geared transmission. By the end of the 1941 model year, the Model LI existed as the only official John Deere industrial tractor in production.

The new Model LI proved itself to be an effective and popular industrial tractor. Like its yellow-painted Model L predecessors, the LI served mainly to mow roadsides

for state and local highway departments, but the tractor also found acceptance in a variety of other roles as well. For instance, it made a handy lot tractor for pulling small items around in tight locations. What's more, the model's relatively low price tag put it within reach of many potential customers. In its first year, the company produced about 340 units of the new model.

Perhaps the reason the LI became so popular as a mower tractor was that it afforded its operator a high degree of visibility. On the small yellow machine, an operator could easily see in front of him or her, immediately behind him or her, and just how close the tires were to fences or other barriers. *Andy Kraushaar*

The LI had a strong launch, but events in Hawaii and overseas would shortly limit its production and sales potential. Little more than six months after the LI's May introduction, the Japanese bombed Pearl Harbor on December 7, 1941, pulling the United States into the Second World War. The war disrupted the national economy in many ways: able-bodied men left farms, offices, and factories to fight; industry shifted production from peacetime goods to war materiel; and rationing of goods such as gas,

tires, aluminum, rubber, and brass left manufacturers without adequate supplies to build or repair their products. Tractor production decreased throughout the nation, though manufacturers continued to produce some models—the nation still had to feed itself, even if many of its farmers had shipped out to fight.

Deere temporarily discontinued some of its tractor models during the war. Such interruptions rarely lasted more than a year per suspended model, but production declined across the board. The

company made 425 Model LI tractors in 1942, but just under 50 in 1943. It built no L or LA models that year. In 1944, Deere & Company didn't build any Model GM or Model H tractors, applying its limited production materials instead to the mid-sized Model B and Model A tractors. Production of the Model B, a very popular agricultural tractor, was down 21 percent during the war years. Compared to these other tractors, the Model LI's production drop of only 14 percent over that period doesn't look too bad.

Without a front-mounted blade, the Model B series Lindeman crawlers could still do a lot. They could plow, they could pull things, and they could certainly turn heads. But whenever these machines came fitted with a front dozer blade, watch out! With that attachment, they pushed themselves into the forests, moving not only logs out of the way but also any reservations customers might have had about using an agricultural tractor for forestry work. *Andy Kraushaar*

Before production ceased in 1946, Deere & Company would produce more than 2,000 Model LI tractors during its six-year production run.

Things started looking more promising for the Allied forces in Europe and even in the Pacific starting in 1944. One result was a slight recovery in tractor production within the United States. For the Model LI, production increased 400 percent over 1943 figures, up from slightly fewer than 50 units to slightly more than 200. The Models L and LA also went back into production, the LA still being available with industrial paint and features.

Deere and other manufacturers made few changes to their products during the war years because of limited supplies and reduced sales. The government had also imposed price freezes on many goods, including tractors, further discouraging new innovations or upgrades—any improvements would go uncompensated in the sales price. And why would a manufacturer want to give its competitors a look at a new innovation before it could benefit from it financially? Behind the scenes, though, many companies continued to research and plan new, improved models. As soon as the economy improved, they would put these ideas into production. Deere's engineers were quietly experimenting with diesel-fueled engines and with hydraulic lift systems, both of which would prove extremely beneficial to the company's industrial tractors in the years ahead.

Even though Lindeman could have converted more Model BR tractors into crawlers than it did, the company opted to convert the BO tractors instead. The move was a smart one, and it certainly helped make the tractors all the more acceptable to the logging industry. The BO featured few obstructions above its hood and elsewhere—a design decision Deere had made when crafting the model to satisfy the needs of an orchard. Those features proved just as beneficial in the forest. *Randy Leffingwell*

Lindeman Puts More John Deere Tractors on Tracks: The BO and BR Lindemans

Fortunately, Deere didn't have to wait until the end of World War II to benefit from the production of a "new" model that would improve Deere's prospects in the industrial tractor market. In 1943, the Lindeman Power Equipment Company of Yakima, Washington, picked up where it had left off back in 1940, when it had converted one Model BI John Deere tractor into a crawler by adding track assemblies to the unit. Deere had terminated production of the Model BI back in mid-1941, but the BR and BO models, which used the same chassis, were still in production. At the time of their release, the BO and BR Lindeman crawlers weren't exactly industrial models, but the market would come to identify and employ tracked tractors as industrial machines. Thus Lindeman was setting a foundation for Deere's future.

Lindeman converted only a handful of the BR tractors into

crawlers, but it converted far more of the BO models with the same track assemblies. By the end of production, Lindeman produced around 1,700 John Deere Model BO crawlers, accounting for nearly one-third of all standard-tread Model B John Deeres produced during those years. Although this is some 300 fewer than total LI production, Lindeman produced its crawlers over a five-year period compared to the LI's six-year run.

Why was the BO Lindeman crawler so successful? It was just the right size, had just the right amount of power, and had just the right price for many, many people. More important, though, the John Deere Model BO Lindeman crawler was versatile. Not only did it perform well in agricultural applications, but it absolutely shone in the logging industry. The tracks of the BO and BR Lindemans worked well in the rough terrain of the forest, terrain that sometimes proved troublesome for rubber-tired two-wheel-drive tractors. The BO and BR Lindeman crawlers could pull logs just fine, and they could also push them. The latter was done via an attached dozer-type blade. And, with that blade, the BO and BR Lindeman crawlers proved their worth in earthmoving applications as well. Those crawlers might not have been industrial yellow, but they proved that they could do the work of tractors that were.

Change in the Postwar Years

Shortly after the war, Deere wound down production of the

The B series Lindeman crawlers pawed their way into industrial markets and became a wonderful foundation on which Deere could expand in the future. The lessons this model and its immediate successors would teach Deere would help the company in producing its first full-fledged bulldozer. *Andy Kraushaar*

Model B and Model H tractors, in addition to the Model L and its derivatives. The L and LI were terminated in June 1946, with the LA following two months later. In mid-January 1947, Deere terminated production of its standard-tread Model B series, even though the row-crop Model Bs continued production after that time. This cut also put an end to both Model BO and BR production, and with it Lindeman's tracked versions of these models.

The Model H, which had no factory-produced standard-tread derivatives or industrial variations, ended production in early February 1947. The H had served as the smallest conventional tricycle-front-end row-crop tractor in Deere's line, and it had been quite popular.

Soon Deere would replace these discontinued tractors with one basic model series. That tractor was already in the works, and it was nearly ready for production.

CHAPTER 3

The Dubuque Answer: Bringing in the New

Deere's Waterloo, Iowa, factory had long been the company's production backbone in the tractor industry. Deere officially entered the tractor market there, first taking over production of the Waterloo Boy models, then eventually moving on to produce tractors bearing the company's own name. Waterloo had tradition, Waterloo was well established. But as the company approached 110 years in business, management decided that it was time to set up another factory, in part to increase and diversify tractor production. The company looked east, approximately 90 miles, to Dubuque. Here, access to the Mississippi River would facilitate receiving and shipping materials, parts, and finished products.

According to Brian R. Alm's book *A History of the John Deere Industrial Equipment Division*, Deere & Company acquired land in Dubuque, Iowa, then broke ground for the new factory in the summer of 1945. The facility, known as Deere's Dubuque Tractor Works, started operation in the fall of 1946. The first tractor produced at Dubuque, a Model M, rolled off the line in April 1947.

The Model M Starts Production

In mid-March 1947, just over one month after the Model H ended production, Deere initiated production of the Model M John Deere. The model featured a "square" engine with a 4x4-inch bore and stroke, giving the unit around 101 cubic inches of displacement. Like the L, the M's engine was of an upright two-cylinder design. But the M was noticeably bigger than the L had been. The new model weighed in at around 2,500 pounds, whereas the L weighed almost exactly half a ton less. Featuring a four-speed transmission with forward speeds ranging from 1.62 to 12 miles per hour, the M was still a very nimble

In 1947, Deere & Company started producing a new line of tractors that would take both the agricultural and industrial tractor markets by storm. With this new line, manufactured at Deere's new facilities in Dubuque, Iowa, the company would solidify its footing in crawler, utility, and industrial tractor production. *Randy Leffingwell*

The Model M John Deere came on the scene partly in response to Ford's successful N series tractors with the Ferguson system. Two keys to the Model M's success were its hydraulic lift system and its utility-type design.

tractor, though, and it was ready to get to work.

When the Model M started production, it certainly had some big shoes to fill. It needed to take up the slack caused by the cancellation of the L, H, and standard-tread B models. How could the Model M series replace so many tractors? The answer lies in the tractor's fundamental design. In many ways, the M was unlike any other single tractor model Deere had ever produced. Yet it derived from a combination of two prior model designs—the Models L and H. The basic Model M actually looked strikingly similar to the

Model L, but it incorporated stylistic features used on Model H series tractors.

The most important thing about the M's design, though, was that it was a utility—all of Deere's previous tractors were not. By definition, the utility tractor's basic configuration was well suited for nearly any agricultural job—from the row-crop work that tractors like the Models L and H had performed, to plowing and hauling jobs for which the standard-tread Model B series tractors were used. And the Model M equaled or topped the power rating of all of its predecessors.

The versatility of the M series tractors made them highly adaptable to industrial applications, and the Model M even proved itself convertible into a tractor designed specifically for industrial use. These tractors were initially used for light jobs, such as mowing. But Deere had more uses in mind. In 1949, Deere started converting the M into new specialized models to fulfill a variety of customer needs. The Model MT, for example, was an M series tractor with a tricycle-row-crop front end, to serve customers who preferred the former model H's configuration over the utility layout. Deere was also hard at work on industrial variants.

The Model MI: Industrial at Last!

Introduced in late 1949, the Model MI featured the same engine used in all of the other M series tractors. What made the MI special was its chassis design. Deere gave the MI a lower center of gravity—important for some industrial jobs—by simply rotating forward by one-quarter turn the drop-box-type housings used on the regular utility version of the Model M. In addition to lowering the tractor's center of gravity, the forward-rotated axle housings also reduced the tractor's wheelbase, helping to give the unit a shorter turning radius. Deere also made yellow the MI's standard color, just as had been the case with Deere's previous official industrial tractor models.

The MI's most important feature wasn't its lowered center of gravity or its shorter turning radius or its yellow color, however. It was its hydraulic system. The Model MI John Deere was the first true John Deere industrial tractor with a sophisticated hydraulic system. Deere had been installing its "Power Lift" and "Powr-Trol" hydraulic systems on its agricultural row-crop tractors for years, but Deere hadn't ever adopted those systems for its industrial tractors. The M series' new hydraulic system—the "Touch-O-Matic" hydraulic system—featured the most precise hydraulic control yet seen on a John Deere tractor. The Touch-O-Matic also benefited from the M's rear implement hitch, much like a three-point hitch. Deere dubbed the M's

The M's utility design meant that it could be used for almost anything, including industrial applications. The tractor could handle many such jobs, but the most predominant industrial-type work the M saw was mowing roadsides, like its predecessors the Model L and LI tractors.

implement-attachment system the "Quik-Tatch," and it allowed operators to hitch up implements much faster than they had ever before been able to do with previous Deere tractors. The MI was an advanced machine, and it performed with style and purpose.

The Model MC: More Industrial than the Industrial?

The original Model M tractor was a suitable replacement for Deere's previous Model BO and BR tractors. But the Model M only replaced the wheeled versions of those models, not the BO and BR Lindeman crawlers. It would take a little time, engineering, and retooling to fill that void. Fortunately, Deere had been working on the

Lindeman replacement even before the M officially began production.

By the time Deere began experimenting with the preproduction Model XM tractors—tractors that would culminate in the Model M—the company was aware of the market's interest in the Lindeman-converted crawler versions of Deere's standard-tread Model B series tractor, particularly the orchard Model BO. Deere also knew that the BO Lindeman crawlers were successful in a variety of different fields, both agricultural (particularly in orchards) and industrial. Terminating the standard-tread B tractors in 1947 would cut off access to those markets by removing the crawler conversion's base model.

While the rear-mounted belt pulley on the Model M did help to expand its uses somewhat, the lift system on the Model M did even more to boost the model's usability and popularity.

But in 1946—prior to both the actual start of Model M production and the termination of the standard-tread Model B tractors—Deere made moves to help ensure that that gap wouldn't remain in Deere's line for long. At that time, Deere shipped one of its preproduction Model XM tractors, XM-17, off to Lindeman to see if it was going to be possible to put the upcoming model on tracks. Lindeman succeeded, and the results were so impressive that Deere & Company decided it was high time to try to purchase the Lindeman Power Equipment Company and

its designs so that Deere could produce crawler tractors under its own management. Deere successfully made the purchase, and the former Lindeman facilities became known as Deere's Yakima Works.

Deere documents indicate that Deere & Company began production at its Yakima Works in 1947. The primary task of the factory there was to produce the track assemblies for the Model M series crawlers, which came to be known as the Model MC. The first MC didn't roll off the line until very late in 1948, on December 28. The first MC received serial number 10001,

starting the 1949 model year production. Deere produced the MC for four model years, terminating manufacture at the close of the 1952 model year. By that time, Deere & Company had produced around 6,300 MCs, almost four times the number of BO Lindeman crawlers.

The Model MC was the first regular production crawler tractor built entirely by Deere & Company, yet it was built in much the same way as the Lindeman units. The base tractor—everything except the track assemblies—was produced at the factory in Dubuque. Deere then shipped the tractors, less wheels, west to Yakima, where that factory added the finishing touch: the track assemblies. Deere & Company often cites 1949 as the year it started producing crawler tractors.

The Model MC Makes Industrial Moves

With the M series tractors—particularly the Models MI and MC—in production, Deere was ready to expand its presence in the industrial marketplace. The staff at the Yakima factory took the lead, developing new attachments and configurations to make the tractor more appealing to a variety of different industries.

Model 1000 Tool Carrier

In 1949, the Yakima plant started producing the Model 1000 tool carrier, which was specifically designed for use on the MC crawlers. Operators could mount the tool carrier onto either the front or the back of the MC, depending on what they wished to attach to the unit. If the tool carrier was mounted on the front of the crawler, the operators could install a dozer blade, converting the MC from a crawler tractor into a bulldozer for traditional earth-moving tasks. Deere also eventually offered a special dozer blade for the

The M's versatile design also gave it lots of potential in industrial applications. Deere & Company produced the Model M in a variety of different configurations to serve industrial as well as agricultural purposes.

Deere's Model MI of 1949 filled the gap created when the company discontinued the smaller Model LI. Like the LI, the MI featured an upright two-cylinder engine, but this tractor had many advantages over its predecessor. *Randy Leffingwell*

One of the most important advantages that the MI had over the LI was its hydraulic system. The MI used the same Touch-O-Matic system used by the basic Model M. With that system, operators could control semi-mounted, rear-mounted, and belly- or side-mounted equipment much more conveniently. *Andy Kraushaar*

Model MC that broadened the ways in which the machine could push dirt and other such materials. Known as the Model 61, this blade could be set at different angles. Operators could also mount the Model 1000 tool carrier on the back of the MC, where the carrier served as a special hitch. With that hitch, any number of implements—including a plow—could be mounted on the tractor.

Use of "Allied Equipment"

Late in the production of the Model MC, Deere approved three new items of "allied equipment" for use with the model. They included a posthole digger and two models of winches that attached to the rear of the tractor. Deere's adoption of such "allied equipment" for use on the MC's progeny would make them among the most useful tractors in the industrial, construction, and forestry markets.

From the operator's perspective, the MI was also far more comfortable than its predecessors. Deere & Company had been striving to make its tractors more operator-friendly for years — a trend that persists to this day — and things just kept getting better and better. *Randy Leffingwell*

The Model 40 Replaces the M Series

Deere & Company ended production of the Model M series tractors in 1953, replacing them at that time with a quite similar tractor, the Model 40 series. Like the M, almost all of the many versions of the 40 could be useful in industrial applications. The 40's engine had the same bore and stroke as the M's, but could be revved 200 rpms faster and had a slightly higher compression ratio. While the M produced a rated 18.15 drawbar and 21.45 PTO horsepower, the 40 was rated at 22.9 horsepower at the drawbar and 25.2 at the PTO. More power meant the 40 found it that much easier to take care of business.

From Yakima to Dubuque: The Model 40-C

The factory at Yakima had put Deere tractors on tracks, even from the beginning. But Yakima, Washington, was quite far away from where Deere started producing the tractors that eventually would receive those tracks. Model MC tractors initially produced at the Dubuque facility had to travel around 1,900 miles west-northwest before they received their own propulsion systems at Yakima. Perhaps that is why Deere decided to shift production of the track systems for the MC's replacement— the Model 40 crawler—from the Yakima facility to Dubuque when the new model started production.

The John Deere Model MI looked to be a stable tractor, and its firm stance with an amazing flexibility in operations set a precedent for future Deere industrials. For instance, the highly popular 440 series John Deere traced its roots directly back to the Model MI. *Randy Leffingwell*

Deere began production of the Model 40 crawler (also known as the Model 40-C) as a 1953 model year product in November 1952. It commenced the model's serial numbers at 60001. Initially, Deere used an undercarriage assembly on the 40-C that was very similar to that of the Model MC. Thus, the very early 1953 model 40-Cs used a three-roller track assembly.

The 40-C Receives More Track Rollers

Not long after production of the 40-C began, however, Deere decided that the three-roller track assembly would not allow the tractor to achieve its full potential. Used in agricultural applications, the MC was nimble and performed well with three rollers. But more and more customers were putting their crawlers to more demanding uses, such as forestry, in uneven terrain. To prepare its new crawler for an upgraded track system, Deere temporarily suspended production of the 40-C beginning on June 1, 1953. A month and a half later, having made the desired changes to the production facilities, Deere resumed production of the 40-C with the next serial number, 62264. From this point onward, the 40-C was no longer available with three-roller assemblies. Instead, the buyer could choose either four- or five-roller assemblies. Deere also offered various sizes of track shoes, including shoes with 10-, 12-, and 14-inch widths.

In rougher terrain, the tracks of the tractor had to climb over things of varying heights with far more

DID YOU KNOW?
DEERE'S "ALLIED EQUIPMENT PROGRAM"

John Deere tractors made use of various pieces of "allied equipment" that improved their versatility and productiveness; Deere documents make that fact very clear. What is far less apparent is the source of this term. Was Allied Equipment an outside organization of suppliers that offered equipment to Deere and perhaps others, or was it a program Deere initiated to describe attachments that would work with its products? In his book, *A History of the John Deere Industrial Equipment Division*, Brian R. Alm first mentions "allied equipment" in all lowercase letters when discussing the use of those items on the Model MC. Shortly thereafter, however, he indicates that there was, indeed, an "Allied Equipment Program."

The name of the Allied Equipment Program might confuse some. For instance, there exist today several independent manufacturers called "Allied Equipment" and a number of modern equipment dealerships named "Allied Equipment." But "Allied Equipment" wasn't either a dealer or a manufacturer who produced items specifically for use on Deere's tractors. Instead, the individual words in the phrase "Allied Equipment Program" exactly describe just what it was. *Allied* is synonymous with the terms *related* or *associated*. And, of course, *equipment* simply means just that—equipment. *Program* in this case clearly means a plan of action. Therefore, Deere's Allied Equipment Program was a program in which Deere & Company authorized various different attachments (produced by outside manufacturers) that could be fitted on (or "teamed up with") its industrial tractors; hence, allied equipment. Alm, who in an interview confirmed that that is pretty much what the Allied Equipment Program was, also indicated that Deere at one time published an Attachment Guide in the program that served as a means to cross-reference outside manufacturers' attachments with the Deere tractors they would work on. What remains unclear regarding the program, however, is exactly when it started and when, if ever, it ended.

regularity than they ever had to do in relatively flat agricultural fields. That meant that the tracks, and thus the tractors, had to go "over center" more often. Shorter tracks didn't have to go very far before they had to go over-center, and they also had to climb up to get to the over-center pivot point quickly. But, as the old saying goes, what goes up must come down. And, in the case of tracks, what goes up quickly must come down quickly, too. So, once the three-roller tracks went over-center, the tracks came back down on the other side quite quickly—and

abruptly, too. Thus, riding over rough terrain on a crawler with short tracks (such as those found on the three-roller MCs and the very early 40-Cs) could be a rather jarring experience. However, with longer tracks, the tractors climbed to the over-center point more gradually, and the tracks came down on the other side more gradually.

For the Model 40-C, the new longer track assemblies didn't just help the unit overcome obstacles; they also helped the model get better traction, both from increased surface area and increased weight.

Not exactly an industrial tractor, the Model MC nevertheless helped Deere gain popularity with those involved in forestry work and earthmoving activities. These tractors were also successful in the more traditional agricultural roles for which they were designed. *Randy Leffingwell*

Allied Equipment for the 40 Series

Over time, Deere approved other pieces of allied equipment for the Model 40 series in addition to those items that had previously been approved for use with the MC (including the Model 61 angling dozer blade). The 40-C could be fitted with an additional winch model, a rear scoop, a post driver, sprayers, and even a log cart. Deere's little 40-C was certainly starting to prove itself in the forestry department and in many other realms, too.

The Model 40 was a good tractor for John Deere, but it, too, had

The Model M series tractors, including the Model MC, shared the same basic styled appearance with most of Deere's other agricultural tractors, including the Models A, B, and G. This design wasn't planned for industrial or forestry work, it seems, but the sheet-metal style certainly didn't inhibit the tractor's abilities in those fields. *Randy Leffingwell*

to come to an end. Deere's termination of Model 40 production on October 17, 1955, however, shouldn't be considered a sad note since the 40 was soon to be replaced with an even better tractor—the Model 420.

The Model 420 Starts Production, Plus an All-New Tractor Size Is Born

Deere & Company released the Model 420 series tractors in November 1955, starting out the 1956 model year. The 420s had larger engines than their predecessor, with a bore 1/4 inch bigger than the one used in the Model 40. This increase bumped displacement from 100.5 inches to about 113.3 inches, while rated rpm remained unchanged. The boost in engine size helped give the 420 a rated belt performance of nearly 25 horsepower, making it just about 3 1/2 horsepower stouter than the Model 40.

Like the Model 40, the 420 could come in a variety of configurations, and all but one of those were primarily agricultural tractors. Strangely enough, the one 420 series tractor that Deere did specifically designate as an industrial model was actually nothing more than a modified version of one of the agricultural 420s.

Deere also introduced an all-new Dubuque-built model in the 1956 model year, the Model 320. Smaller than the 420, the 320 shared many features with its big brother that made it appealing for industrial customers. Deere, however, had bigger industrial hopes for the 420.

The first crawler tractor model built exclusively by Deere, the MC wasn't perfect as a bulldozer or for other forestry operations, but one must keep in mind that the model wasn't designed to do those things. Deere soon recognized the potential these models had in those markets, however, so the company made sure that the MC's progeny were better designed for use therein. The results were amazing. *Randy Leffingwell*

This Model MC John Deere sits aside piles of stumps that it may very well have bulldozed there. While Deere did have a few earlier tractors converted into crawlers, the MC put the company firmly on the crawler map. Its track-based concept would be the foundation for many of Deere's future industrial machines, ranging from bulldozers to excavators. *Andy Kraushaar*

DID YOU KNOW?
TRACK ASSEMBLIES AND TRACK ROLLERS

To understand why Deere & Company decided to increase the number of track rollers on the Model 40-C, one must understand what purpose track rollers serve in a crawler's track assemblies. Here is a brief description of how track assemblies work:

If one were to strip a track assembly of its tracks and the lower track rollers and the upper support rollers, what would be left would to some degree resemble—with a minor stretch of one's imagination—a regular, everyday wheel tractor. On each side of a crawler, the heart of the track assembly consists of a track frame (which runs almost the entire length of each track). In a way, the track frame serves as a second—or possibly an extended—chassis frame for the base tractor. That track frame has "wheels" of sorts attached to it, one at the front of the frame and one at the back. Since there are two sides to most crawlers' track frames, there are therefore two of those wheels at the back of the tractor, and two of those wheels at the front of the tractor—just like on a regular wheeled farm tractor.

The rear "wheel" on each track frame works very much like each rear wheel works on most common wheeled farm tractors. On a crawler, however, that "rear wheel" isn't called a rear wheel; instead, it's called the "drive sprocket." Like the rear wheel of a regular farm tractor, the drive sprocket is attached to an axle that runs out of the final drives (or "rear end") of the tractor, attached directly to the bull gear. This drive sprocket operates much like the

rear drive wheels of a wheeled tractor. Instead of turning a wheel that has a tire attached to it, however, the drive sprocket has cogs, or teeth, that mesh into the actual tracks. Thus, when the drive sprocket turns, it moves the tracks in whichever direction the drive sprocket is turning.

The front "wheel" on each track frame does resemble the front wheels located at the front of a regular wheeled tractor, but they function in different ways. On a wheeled tractor, the front wheels often are connected to a steering gear and are capable of turning right or left; their movement is used to change the direction of travel for the tractor in most cases. On a crawler, however, the "front wheels" (which are really called "front idlers") can't turn directions; they are "idle" since they always point straight forward.

Operators change a crawler's direction of travel with a set of levers that serve as controls for a turning system that operates similarly to the independent rear-wheel brake systems found on agricultural tractors. That feature is sometimes used even to turn wheeled tractors when soil conditions do not provide enough traction for the pivoting front wheels to do the job alone. For example, engaging the right brake slows or stops the right rear wheel, while the left rear wheel continues traveling at the same speed. This turns the tractor to the right. The same principles apply to crawler tractors, but they must rely on that system to turn, not just use it as a supplement.

With the drive and turning functions in mind, we can move on to the tracks themselves. The tracks on each side of the crawler tractor wrap around the front of the

front idlers and the back of the drive sprockets. The endless tracks extend between both of them with little slack or "play."

Track rollers are wheels attached to the bottom of the track frame and placed between the rear drive sprockets and the front idlers. Their purpose is to support the tractor as it moves over uneven terrain and to limit stress on the tracks. A tractor without track rollers could move over level ground with just the drive sprockets and idlers, but if it went over a ridge, the long portion of unsupported track between these points would bear the full weight of the tractor, placing too much strain on the tracks.

Another type of roller, known as a carrier (or support) roller, is mounted to the top of the track frame. Its purpose is to support the track itself between the idler and drive sprocket. Because the track weighs significantly less than the tractor itself, fewer support rollers are required. The Model 40-C with five track rollers uses only one support roller per side.

What determines the number of track rollers needed in a track assembly? The most important determining factor is the length of the tracks. Short tracks need few rollers, whereas longer tracks require more. Thus, when Deere decided it wanted to lengthen the tracks on the Model 40-C, it only made sense that the company added either one or two track rollers (depending upon the overall length of the tracks) to do the job right.

The basic design of track systems hasn't changed much since the 1940s, although manufacturers such as Deere & Company continue to find ways to improve the performance and extend the life of these track systems.

While it is true that most bulldozers and crawlers weigh more than wheeled tractors, in many cases they apply less weight per square inch to the ground. This is because a crawler's tracks distribute the tractor's weight over a much greater surface area than do the tires on its wheeled counterparts. *Randy Leffingwell*

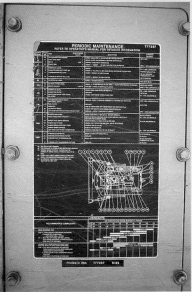

Since the tracks on bulldozers and other crawlers are almost always down in the dirt, they typically require far more maintenance attention than do the wheels on regular wheel tractors. In certain conditions, however, the performance of track-driven machines is far superior to that of wheel tractors, making the added maintenance demands justifiable.

The Model 420-I: One Industrial Version

To make the Model 420-I, Deere basically just converted the row-crop Model 420-W tractor. The 420-I even had a supplemental designation of "Special Utility," showing the model's utility-based roots. Deere produced only about 250 or so Model 420-I tractors, the majority of which were painted yellow.

Interestingly, the Model 420-I wasn't the most successful industrial tractor in the 420 series lineup. Now, wait a minute, you say, wasn't the Model 420-I the only industrial version of the 420 series? Yes. But nearly all of the many agricultural derivatives of the 420 found themselves performing industrial duties at some point. The only obvious exception to that generalization was the Model 420-V vegetable tractor, which likely had little if any appeal to industrial customers because it was highly specialized for use in cultivating fields of vegetables and other bedded crops.

The Model 420-C: A Crawler That Wore Many Hats

The most obvious 420 series agricultural tractor put to industrial use was the Model 420-C crawler. Like the later versions of its predecessor, the 420-C came on either four- or five-roller tracks. The five-roller 420-C John Deeres, on the basis of their longer tracks, found themselves more comfortable performing industrial tasks than their four-roller brothers. But customers

Starting with the Model 40-C, people working in almost every field where tractors were used began to know Deere crawlers. The biggest turning point for this model came when Deere made the unit's track assemblies longer, which increased stability and improved performance in other ways. *Randy Leffingwell*

found both models useful for industrial-related applications.

Logging Attachments for the Model 420-C

The Model 420-C didn't differ much from the 40-C that preceded it, but Deere did make an even greater number of attachments available for the new model. As a result, its ability to perform industrial tasks far surpassed that of the older model. Deere started producing three all-new items in all-new forestry-related categories specifically for the Model 420-C; those included the Model 24 scarifier, the Model 600 brush and rock rake, and the Model 100 log arch.

Other Industrial-Capable 420-C Attachments

The 420-C could certainly fill industrial shoes beyond the forest, too. Another new Deere-produced item slated for use with the 420-C was the Model 90 loader, though it is unclear whether Deere started producing that item before or after the 420-C terminated production. The company also made a variety of additional dozer blades for the versatile 420-C. The crawler could still use the Model 61 angling dozer blade, but operators could also couple the 420-C with Deere's new Model 62 and Model 63 blades, both of which had a side-to-side tilt feature in addition to the angling feature. Operators could also use Deere's Model 602 bulldozer blade with the 420-C.

Perhaps the most important attachment that Deere & Company started producing for the 420-C was yet another bulldozer blade. That blade, the Model 64, became the first "all-hydraulic" dozer blade available on a John Deere tractor. Interestingly, some operators (and sometimes even Deere) didn't refer to tractors fitted with the dozer blades as the tractor model, fitted with the blade model (e.g., a Model 420-C with a Model 62 blade). Instead, they often simply referred to the units by the blade model, for example, a Model 62 bulldozer. The same practice of calling the crawler-plus-attachment by the attachment model name was common for almost every other Deere-produced attachment coupled with such John Deere crawler tractors.

The Model 420-U Utility Tractor: A Two-Field Tractor

The Model 420-C wasn't the only agricultural 420 series tractor used for industrial purposes. Indeed, of all the agricultural 420 series tractors, the Model 420-U utility tractor was perhaps the most active agricultural tractor in terms of industrial-type jobs. Deere advertised that "ITS USES ARE VARIED AND PROSPECTS ARE MANY." To provide support for that claim, Deere's advertising

pamphlet devoted two full pages to outlining many different applications that the tractor could perform, as well as indicating what equipment was necessary to perform those applications. Here is a list of some of the jobs that Deere advertised that the 420 Utility could perform:

SOME ADVERTISED USES FOR THE MODEL 420 UTILITY

Excavating for and/or installing foundations, pools, basements, patios, manholes, etc.
Installing and repairing water lines
Installing gas lines
Draining septic tanks, storm sewers, sewer lines, sumps, cesspools, etc.
Handling materials for various applications
Grading grounds for building sites, etc.
Removing brush, trees, stumps, or debris
Laying cement for curbs, sidewalks, driveways, foundations, etc.
Repairing cement constructions
Moving cement foundations, etc.
Removing cement when needed
Generating electrical power
Cleaning up building sites
Cleaning streets, sidewalks, etc.
Clearing land after construction
Building fences
Building terraces
Digging graves
Planting grass, trees, shrubs, etc.
Spraying of fertilizers, pesticides, etc.
Mowing roadsides, parks, golf courses, etc.
Removing snow
And more

The Model 420 Utility tractor could only perform all of those industrial applications with the aid of attached or otherwise related equipment of some sort. Those

things, according to Deere's literature for the 420 Utility, included the following items:

SOME INDUSTRIAL EQUIPMENT FOR THE MODEL 420 UTILITY

Backhoe
Straight dozer blade
Angle dozer blade
Center-mounted blade
Backfill blade
Front-end loader
Sawmobile
Scara-scraper
Wheel scraper
Posthole digger
Centrifugal pump
Post driver
Redi-mixer
Trenchers
Landscape rake
Sweeper
Mounted sweeper
Cement breaker
Rear-mounted generator
Reel mower
Hydraulic mower
Gyramor rotary cutter
Center-mounted rotary cutter
Rear roller
Fireline plow
Boom sprayer
Boomless sprayer
Seeder-pulverizer
Rear seeder
Tree tiller
Transplanter
Crane attachments
Forklift
Scarifier
V-type snowplow
Angle snowplow
Snow blower

Overall, Deere & Company approved nearly 50 pieces of allied equipment (in addition to the Deere-produced attachments) for use with the 420 series tractors. The 420-U and the 420-C used the majority of those pieces.

The Model 420 Forklifts

The John Deere Model 420 could also be converted into yet another unique machine: a forklift. In cooperation with the Holt Equipment Company of Independence, Oregon, Deere & Company had a handful of its Model 420-U utility tractors modified to accept Holt's Model 3-T forklift attachment. Since the forklift attached to the rear of the tractor, the operator's station had to be drastically modified. In addition, the rear wheels and tires of the unit were changed to a much smaller size from the regular agricultural type. The heart of the tractor remained much the same, however, the conversion to a forklift not requiring any engine modifications.

Models 330 and 430 Introduced

To replace the Models 320 and 420, Deere introduced the Models 330 and 430 for the 1958 model year. While Deere didn't specifically produce a 330-I or a 430-I tractor, versions of both could be ordered painted industrial yellow and fitted with special attachments. The industrialized utility versions of the tractors shone in mowing roadsides and the like, while the 430 series also offered a crawler that pawed its way into industrial customers' hearts, just like the previous Deere crawlers had done. As popular as that tractor, the Model 430-C, was, it wasn't the most unique 430 intended for industrial use.

Model 430 Forklifts

Few particulars are known about the John Deere Model 420

tractors fitted with the Holt 3-T forklifts, but more information is fortunately available on that unit's replacement. When the Model 430 John Deere replaced the 420, it became the basis for the John Deere-Holt forklifts. The John Deere 430 Holt 3-T forklifts (sometimes known as the Model F-3 forklifts) saw only limited production, but they are important nevertheless.

A critical fact to keep in mind when talking about and picturing the John Deere-Holt forklifts is that what normally would be considered the "front" of the tractor was actually the back of the forklift unit. The John Deere 430 Holt 3-T forklift thus used 8.25x15-inch eight-ply dual front wheels (also called the drive wheels) and smaller 6.50x10 ten-ply rear wheels (also called the pivot wheels).

Overall, John Deere 430 Holt 3-T forklifts were very versatile. They had a vertical lift of 9 1/2 feet, and the forklift assembly could be tilted backward up to 9 degrees from vertical (usually used to lift materials and while transporting materials at an elevated position) and forward up to 10 degrees from vertical (usually used to leave materials in a particular position or when first moving into position to prepare to lift the items). The unit used two 3x55-inch lift cylinders and two 3x12 5/16-inch tilt cylinders. Deere advertised that, when the center of the load being lifted was 20 inches from the face of the tines, this unit had a total lift capacity of 6,000 pounds, or 3 tons. Deere promoted these machines for work in factories, foundries,

airports, canneries, warehouses, dockyards, wrecking yards, lumberyards, and at sawmills. In those places, these forklifts could perform a wide variety of tasks, including the following:

SOME ADVERTISED USES FOR THE 430 HOLT FORKLIFTS

Stacking of:
Logs
Lumber
Crates
Cases
Sacked Goods
Loading of:
Logs
Lumber
Salvage
Handling of:
Logs
Lumber
Cargo
Baggage
Restaurant Supplies
Castings
Barrels
Beams
Loading and Unloading:
Trucks
Freight/Flatcars

Six thousand pounds was a lot of weight to lift. To do so, the John Deere 430 Holt 3-T combination weighed considerably more than its agricultural counterpart. The 430 Holt 3-T weighed nearly 7,950 pounds—roughly 100 pounds more than Deere & Company's stalwart Model 830-I industrial tractor. Compare that with the average 3,000 pounds of the regular 430 wheel-type agricultural tractors, and the weight difference and lifting capacity of the forklift version is quite amazing. Even the five-roller Model 430-C crawler tractor didn't weigh nearly as much as the forklift version did; the crawler tipped the scales at only around 4,700 pounds.

The Holt conversions of the Models 420 and 430 weren't the only forklifts one could obtain on those models, however. Deere approved the Blackwelder Multi-Purpose AG-60 forklift for use with those models as well. The company also approved that forklift for the John Deere Model 40, though curiously not until it had terminated production of that tractor. The Blackwelder unit had a lift capacity of 2,500 pounds, and could be used in various guises other than a forklift. It was available with either 42- or 48-inch forks, a lift boom, a loader bucket, and even a dozer blade. One manufacturer—Superior Equipment of Wheeling, Illinois—even made loader attachments that could be converted into forklifts for the 420 and 430 series John Deere tractors. The Superior Model H-228S, H-128S, K-218S, and K-118S loaders would fit Deere's 420-U and 430-U tractors, while the Superior H-228I and H-128I loaders would fit the 420-W and 430-W John Deeres. All of these loaders could be fitted with manure forks, dirt plates, material buckets, front bulldozers, crane booms, and even forklifts. Deere & Company also approved the use of Henry Manufacturing Company's Model TL-4200 forklift with the John Deere Model 430-U tractors.

Setting the Stage for an Industrial Revolution

The Dubuque-built John Deere tractors of the late 1940s and the

While Deere industrials had been fitted with crane attachments in the past, never before had there been a John Deere made specifically to work as a forklift. The John Deere Holt 3-T forklifts, based on the John Deere Model 420 and 430 tractors, did just that. *Deere & Company Archives*

entire 1950s excelled in many fields, including industrial applications. They had helped establish Deere & Company as a producer of highly adaptable tractors that could satisfy many different industrial needs. Meanwhile,

Deere had another series in production that was solidifying its reputation in the heavy industrial field. With that, Deere brought the second blow for a one-two punch that set the stage for an industrial revolution.

CHAPTER 4

Heavyweight Moves

Waterloo is where Deere tractor production started, and Waterloo certainly seemed to get it right, right from the start. The tractors produced there largely fulfilled the goals their designers had in mind for them. They were tough machines, and they were highly versatile in many cases. And, since Waterloo did so many things right, they kept doing many of those same things—after all, "if it ain't broke, don't fix it!" Waterloo's consistency, however, should not be confused with a lack of innovation. At Waterloo, Deere did *many* innovative things. This was the place where Deere's Powr-Trol hydraulic system originated, where Deere introduced live hydraulics on its Model H, where Deere's Roll-O-Matic came to life, and where Deere started producing its styled tractors. More notable and important than any of those accomplishments, though, was this: Waterloo introduced diesel fuel to the wheel-tractor market. The wheel tractor that Deere first introduced with a diesel engine did two important things for the company: It set the stage for broad application of diesel-fueled wheel tractors, and it also helped the company establish its heavy industrial line—a class of machines that would become closely associated with construction activities such as road building in the near future.

The Model R John Deere Introduced

The tractor model that started all this was the Model R John Deere, a tractor that Deere released in the 1949 model year. The R was a big, heavy, stout tractor, but it also proved that brutes aren't necessarily dumb. The R served as an expression of the minds of Deere's engineers. And those engineers brought a very intelligent idea to life in the engine of the Model R. The result made the R's engine quite different from any other engine ever installed in a regular-production John Deere tractor.

Many of Deere's prior engines had started on gasoline and then switched to some lower-grade fuel, such as kerosene. The R's engine—a horizontal two-cylinder unit—ran exclusively on diesel. To start it, Deere engineers mated it to a smaller, gasoline engine (often called a "pony motor"). This engine started easily and then turned a gear on the main engine's flywheel to get it started. The smaller engine was then shut down. This

The Model R came to life just in time for Deere's industrial program. Even though the model wasn't designed specifically for industrial use, its power, dependability, sturdiness, size, and impressive fuel economy were just the things many industrial customers wanted in a tractor. *Randy Leffingwell*

Most Model R John Deeres toiled away doing what this one is doing—plowing. The R had sufficient power to pull about three or four plow bottoms (depending upon the soil type), but that power could be used to pull other things as well. And that's exactly what the R and many of its descendants wound up doing for industrial jobs, especially for road building.

system provided for quick, sure starts, and allowed for separate fuel systems unique to each engine. Most important, it provided a very effective means to use the more economical diesel fuel.

The Diesel Fuel Experiment

Deere engineers first started experimenting with diesel engines way back in 1935. That is about the same time that Deere approached Caterpillar with the idea of granting that company the sole rights to distribute Deere's industrial wheel tractors and related equipment. Whether Caterpillar somehow inspired Deere's decision to start experimenting with diesel is not

known, though that company had been working with the fuel for several years by that time—Caterpillar had diesel-powered crawlers in production as early as 1931, and by 1935 had a variety of different model sizes in production powered by diesel engines (with gasoline counterparts in most cases). It's possible that Deere decided to start experimenting with diesel after seeing the success Caterpillar was having with the fuel.

The reason Deere started the diesel project is not entirely clear, but the decision likely had nothing at all to do with Caterpillar. Two things support that claim. For one, Deere undoubtedly already knew

The R's controls were simple, yet effective. Certainly, in most ways the R was all business, another fact that made this stout agricultural model appealing to industrial customers. *Randy Leffingwell*

This 1952 Model R—actually an experimental Model RI industrial—shows off its long frame. Deere had to make the Model R long in part to hold its gargantuan engine. Furthermore, if it were much shorter, the front end might have gotten light in a hard pull. *Randy Leffingwell*

DID YOU KNOW?
THE ADVANTAGES OF DIESEL FUEL

Why was the emergence of diesel fuel usage so important for Deere & Company? For heavy jobs—such as those that tractors and other machines endure in many industrial, construction, and logging applications—diesel fuel has many advantages over gasoline. Those same advantages help explain why today almost all semi trucks that crisscross this country every day use diesel fuel as well. They, like industrial tractors, have a big load on their shoulders, and diesel serves as one of the best fuels in those conditions.

Unlike gasoline (a highly volatile fuel), diesel fuel doesn't just propel engines—it also acts as a sort of lubricant. Thus, the cylinder walls and piston rings in diesel engines don't wear out as quickly as they do in gasoline engines. Diesel engines also don't require the presence of many things that gasoline engines need to operate—things like ignition-system components, including sparkplugs, sparkplug wires, and a magneto or distributor with coils. Thus, diesel engines don't require a constant supply of electrical/battery power to continue operating. So when one couples the lubrication characteristics of diesel fuel with the greatly reduced number of parts needed to operate diesel engines, it is no surprise that diesel engines tend to have a much longer life than their gasoline counterparts.

Diesel engines also tend to operate more efficiently than gasoline engines.

When Rudolph Diesel applied for a patent for his new engine in 1893, he indicated that he intended this new design to replace those of the steam engine and other internal combustion engines of the time. It's somewhat surprising that the diesel engine really didn't totally replace both gasoline and steam engines, as the diesel engine indeed proved itself to be exceptionally efficient in comparison. In early tests, the diesel engine operated at higher than 25 percent efficiency. At that time, the best gasoline engines could only operate at around 20 percent efficiency, while steam engines featured an even lower efficiency rating of around 10 percent.

As time passed, the diesel engine proved its superior efficiency over and over again. In agricultural realms, perhaps the best source one can use to further illustrate the efficiency of the diesel engine is the Nebraska Tractor Tests. Those tests, conducted on site at the University of Nebraska in Lincoln, Nebraska, did far more than just test the power of the tractors being tested—the tests also measured and recorded horsepower hours per gallon of fuel burned for each tractor. Diesel fuel made its mark quickly after being introduced in tractors. For instance, in 1933, Caterpillar's Model Seventy-Five diesel set an all-time fuel economy record at the Nebraska Tractor Tests, rating 14.26 horsepower hours per gallon of diesel. At that time, the fuel economy record for gasoline stood at only 10.14 horsepower hours per gallon, set by the Minneapolis Threshing Machine Company's Model 39-57 back in

1929. Similarly, the fuel economy record for kerosene in 1933 was only 11.36 horsepower hours per gallon, a record also set in 1929 by the Case Model C. Today, the kerosene fuel economy record is still the same as it was then, and the gasoline fuel economy record—even though it has been gradually climbing—still hasn't reached the economy level that diesel fuel reached way back in 1933. Today, diesel still reigns king in the fuel economy records for tractors, besting 18 horsepower hours per gallon.

Despite the numerous advantages of diesel engines, they do have their limitations. For instance, diesel fuel, unlike gasoline or LP gas, can be difficult to ignite at low temperatures. But operators can still start and use diesel fuel-powered machines in extremely cold climates with a little help from isolated heat. Glow plugs, engine block heaters, oil pan heaters, and water system "tank" heaters all serve as ways to help warm up diesel engines so that they may be started with ease. Diesel engines also use special injectors that can be quite difficult, if not impossible, for "shade tree" mechanics to properly repair; therefore, many tractor collectors still prefer gasoline-powered tractors over diesel-powered models. But operators who heavily use and properly maintain their tractors find diesel to be a superior fuel with far more benefits than gasoline engines can boast.

---

about diesel fuel and diesel engines (they had been around since the late 1800s), even though they were not yet highly popular. But Deere likely recognized the numerous advantages that diesel fuel had over gasoline and similar fuels.

The other thing that seems to indicate that Deere's diesel project had little if anything to do with Caterpillar's experience in the field is that Deere didn't jump right into diesel engine production. Instead, Deere & Company

spent 14 painstaking years experimenting with diesel and trying to understand and perfect diesel engines. Finally, in 1949, Deere was satisfied with what it had engineered, and the John Deere Model R hit the market. And it's

Tracing its roots back to the Model R, the Model 820 John Deere proved itself capable of performing extremely heavy jobs. It quickly became popular not just with large-scale farmers but also with industrial customers. The 820 could pull among the heaviest machines of its time, from sheep's foots to scrapers. *Andy Kraushaar*

no surprise that Deere entered the diesel fuel market setting a diesel fuel economy record at the Nebraska Tractor Tests. In 1949, the brand-new John Deere R operated at 17.35 horsepower hours per gallon, beating the previous record by an impressive difference—more than 1 1/2 horsepower hours per gallon.

The Model R had even more significance than just introducing to Deere's line the fuel that would sweep its way through the industrial field. Many heavy construction jobs had to be performed by machines that were brutes on all levels, and the John Deere Model R fit the bill perfectly. First, the R was a brute in its basic chassis design. The massive tractor tipped the scales at around 7,400 pounds, and

Like its predecessors, the Model 830 John Deere could pull double duty with relative ease. Even though Deere did offer a specifically designed Model 830-I industrial tractor, the basic agricultural model seen here could perform many industrial tasks with little or no modification. The 830 could readily leave the fields behind and start sculpting roads and building foundations with just a moment's notice. *Andy Kraushaar*

that's before operators stacked on additional weights (and many operators did just that!). And, since the model only came in one basic standard-tread form, the R had hardly any components that were weaker extensions of the basic unit. Thus, everything on the R was necessary, and Deere designed all those things with a no-frills approach (even though operator comfort didn't get ignored). But the R wasn't just a brute in stature—its engine was capable of delivering brute power. The tractor's 416-ci powerplant could produce around 51 horsepower, and with the tractor's firm grip on the ground beneath it, 45 of that 51 horsepower effectively expressed itself via the tractor's drawbar. Indeed, the R was one big, stout tractor—just what industrial contractors needed to power through the tough jobs. They put the R to hard use and found it effective for their work, even though Deere had marketed the R more as an agricultural tractor.

When Deere released the Model R, the company knew it had one brawny tractor on its hands. And there was a significant demand for just that. For farmers, Rs plowed and plowed and plowed (among other things). But road construction workers found the R useful as well. For them, the R pulled sheep's foot rollers, scrapers, water wagons, and almost anything else that was heavy.

Numbers Replace the Letters: The Model 80 Introduced

The Model R couldn't stay in production forever, mainly

DID YOU KNOW?
DIESEL FUEL ECONOMY AND JOHN DEERE TRACTORS

Today, diesel fuel's importance to agriculture cannot be underestimated. Since diesel really started proving its efficiency back in the 1930s and 1940s, the fuel has gained much popularity. And, even though diesel engines haven't totally replaced gasoline engines, diesel-powered tractors are now in much more regular use than their gasoline or even LP-powered counterparts.

Deere & Company did much to help establish diesel fuel as the top choice for tractors—whether agricultural or industrial—and Deere did so very early, in part by consistently producing tractors that set new records for fuel economy. As mentioned, the Model R diesel set a fuel economy record at the Nebraska Tractor Tests in 1949. Then in 1954, the John Deere Model 70 beat the R's old record, rating 17.74 horsepower hours per gallon of diesel fuel. The next year, the R's replacement, the Model 80 John Deere, topped the R's previous performance of 17.35 horsepower hours per gallon, but fell short of setting the record then held by the 70. The 80 came in with 17.58 horsepower hours per gallon—still very impressive, but not quite the record. But the Model 70's record wouldn't stand for very long. Deere & Company bested itself yet again in 1956, when the 70's replacement—the Model 720 John Deere—set a new record, operating at 17.97 horsepower hours per gallon.

The 720's record lasted a long, long time. Over a quarter of a century later, though, that record finally was topped. But it took another John Deere tractor to do it. This time, in 1983, the John Deere Model 1650 set the new record at 18.64 horsepower hours per gallon. That performance didn't just beat the old record—it slaughtered it. Deere & Company had proven itself and diesel fuel once again.

The Model R's engine was formidable at 416 cubic inches, but its replacement — the Model 80 — would boast an even larger powerplant of 471.5 cubes. *Randy Leffingwell*

The Model 830-I with Hancock scraper looked strikingly similar to the Model 840 with John Deere 400 scraper seen here, and rightfully so. After all, the 840 was based on that only slightly earlier model. *Randy Leffingwell*

because Deere kept improving the model series with even better features. By 1955, Deere & Company had made so many changes to the series that the company deemed it fitting to release a new model to replace the R altogether. Thus, Deere released the Model 80 John Deere in 1955, and from that time on Deere's heavyweight tractors would no longer have basic letter model designations.

The Model 80 John Deere soon found itself doing the same kinds of things that the R had done for the same kinds of people. But the 80 had a number of improvements over the R, all of which made the model more fitting for both agricultural and industrial operations. For instance, the Model 80 proved

itself even more fuel-efficient than the R had been, beating the R's record by nearly 1 horsepower hour per gallon. What's more, the more efficient 80 had a much bigger fuel tank—32 1/2 gallons, compared to the R's 22 gallons. Thus, the 80 could keep working longer than the R could without having to be refueled. Such considerations were important to operators trying to get the highest production out of their workday. The 80 also had a bigger engine than its predecessor. Deere increased the bore from 5.75 inches (which had been the R's bore) to 6.125 inches, a move that boosted the 80's total engine displacement by 55.5 cubic inches over the R's and, not surprisingly,

also caused the tractor's horsepower ratings to skyrocket. The 80 could produce more than 67 PTO horsepower and nearly 62 drawbar horsepower, topping the R's performance by roughly 16 horsepower in both categories. Additionally, the 80 featured a six-speed transmission that offered a greater range of speeds than did the R's five-speed unit. The 80 also featured more options, including power steering and a live PTO.

The Model 820 Takes Over

When Deere released the Model 820 in 1956 to replace the Model 80, the company revealed a tractor that was even more powerful and even more effective in industrial applications. The new model's increase in horsepower was important for the industrial realm as well as the agricultural, but that move wasn't the most significant one Deere made with the 820 to influence the industrial market.

Model 820s with Hancock Scrapers

With the 820, Deere & Company officially acknowledged the fact that this series of tractor was quite popular for industrial applications by making the model available in an all-yellow paint scheme with black trim. A handful of these tractors also found themselves pulling scrapers and playing in the dirt with regularity. The Hancock Manufacturing Company of Lubbock, Texas, built these self-loading hydraulic elevating scrapers, which had a 7.5-cubic-yard capacity.

The 830 Supplants the 820

In 1958, Deere & Company introduced the Model 830 to replace the 820. The John Deere 830 tractor didn't feature any improvements that had a noticeable effect on horsepower ratings when compared with the Model 820. As a result, Deere didn't even bother to submit the tractor to the University of Nebraska Tractor Tests. But for many reasons the 830 proved to be far more popular in both the agricultural and industrial fields than the 820 had been. And even though Deere was naturally pleased when a new model was more popular than its predecessor, the company had far more reasons to be tickled with the reception that the Model 830 received. Deere felt confident that, with the customers' acceptance of the new look of the 830 and other -30 series tractors, customers would like the strikingly similar looks of the surprise Deere was preparing to spring on the tractor industry.

The -30 series John Deere two-cylinder tractors definitely had class. They all featured smoother lines and curves, including the sleek hood sides that gently sloped down from the rear to the front of the hood. And those hood sides stood out even more than the get-your-attention hood sides on the -20 series Deere tractors. Both model series featured John Deere yellow

hood sides, but the -30 series tractors' hood sides grabbed the attention of onlookers more readily—the smooth lines contributed greatly to producing that effect. Overall, the -30 series served as a great transition model series between the -20 series and the New Generation tractors.

Despite its bulky size and stalwart attitude, the 830 was just as classy as all the other -30 series Deere two-cylinder tractors. And the astounding aesthetics of the 830 didn't supplant functionality. The 830 remained exceptionally functional, effective, efficient, reliable, and consequently popular with customers. Like its predecessors, the 830 could take a beating, and it could power through some pretty tough jobs, too. It was a get-down-and-dirty tractor, and a pretty one at that. Thus, operators were comfortable using it for many heavy-duty industrial applications.

The Model 830-I Introduced

Deere knew that the 830 descended from a line of tractors that had proven themselves very capable and even quite popular performing industrial duties, despite their basic model designations and intended agricultural design. Deere had been making moves ever since the Model R was in production to acknowledge that acceptance and even to promote it to some degree. But so far, Deere

hadn't made the R's descendants officially available in industrial configurations. That changed with the Model 830.

Deere made the Model 830 Industrial an official separate model in the company's lineup. Not surprisingly, the 830-I came standard with an industrial yellow paint scheme. The regular John Deere green and John Deere yellow paint scheme as used on the agricultural Model 830 could be had for no additional cost; other colors were available upon request, but they came at an extra price. The 830-I could also come with a variety of tire sizes and styles. They included 14-34 and 15-34 six-ply tires, two styles of 18-26 eight-ply tires (including the bar-type tread as commonly used on agricultural models and nondirectional-type tread, which came in handy in a variety of industrial applications), and grader-type ten-ply 18-26 tires.

The 830 Industrial was, according to Deere literature, "a tractor than can cut operating costs and earn bigger profits in earthmoving, land leveling, strip mining, dam building, city snow removal, and many other jobs that require dependable power and durability." Like the 820, Deere offered the 830-I teamed up with a Hancock scraper. It was a great combination, yet it wasn't as good as things would soon be.

CHAPTER 5

Deere's Industrial Division is Born

One of the most significant years in the history of John Deere industrials is 1956. Not only did at least two very important John Deere industrial tractors come out that year, but it was also the year that Deere established a sales department concerned solely with the company's light industrial equipment. As a result, Deere started keeping separate records for the sale of its industrial machinery that year. Deere industrials were finally getting the attention they deserved.

Since 1956 is the first year that Deere clearly considered its industrial production and sales totally separate from agricultural production and sales, many consider 1956 as the official beginning point of Deere's Industrial Division. Whether or not Deere actually started calling it that at the time is unclear, however. Deere's own statements indicate that the start date of the Industrial Division is a foggy issue even within the company. For instance, a recent Deere document states that "John Deere's Construction Equipment Division was established in the mid-1950s." The year 1956

seems a logical starting date for Deere's Industrial Division, all things considered.

The year 1958 also would be a logical date for the start of Deere's Industrial Division, and for good reason. The most compelling reason is that Deere came out with two new industrial tractors that year. Former Deere employee Brian R. Alm remembers that Deere employees often had discussions trying to decide when the start date for the Industrial Division really was, so it's no surprise that this issue has no clear answer.

Deere's industrial activity for 1956 was certainly a tough act to follow, but Deere proved itself up to the challenge in 1957. According to *A History of the John Deere Industrial Equipment Division* by Brian R. Alm, the company took 15 of its tractors to the Chicago Road Show in Chicago's International Amphitheater. It was the first time Deere made a presentation at the Chicago Road Show, and it was the first time since the 1936 National Road Show in Cleveland, Ohio, that Deere

By the mid-1950s, Deere & Company had already made significant progress in its production of industrial tractors and machines, and the company would make many more advances throughout the rest of the decade — from new models to new company organization — that would help set the stage for the 1960s, yet another decade in which Deere would make history.

DEERE TRADEMARK LOGO CORNER:
THE 1956 VERSION

Usually, when Deere & Company makes a change in its John Deere trademark logo, the change occurs in conjunction with or in relation to some changes within the company. So it comes as no surprise that Deere & Company altered its trademark logo in 1956, doing away with the design the company had adopted just six years before.

The 1950 Deere trademark logo had certainly been an interesting change from prior marks. By 1950, Deere & Company had, indeed, made great strides in establishing itself as one of the most innovative farm machinery companies. And even though Deere eliminated the words "THE TRADE MARK OF QUALITY MADE FAMOUS BY GOOD IMPLEMENTS" beginning with its 1937 trademark logo, the company apparently again felt some need to emphasize the quality of its products in that logo. Thus, for the 1950 version, Deere added the words "QUALITY FARM EQUIPMENT" in a solid colored-in section at the bottom of the logo, a section that could be likened to the ground beneath the famous leaping deer. Those words replaced the words "MOLINE, ILL.", which had previously been used to point out the headquarters for the company. Even though Moline was still important for the company then (just as it is today), Deere's scope had extended far beyond Moline, Illinois, by 1950. Indeed, by that time the company had its headquarters at Moline

and factories at both Waterloo and Dubuque in Iowa, among other important facilities across the United States. The 1950 logo also featured a border that had a curved top and bottom with straight sides; the name "JOHN DEERE" appeared parallel to the top curve, just inside the border and just above the leaping deer logo.

By 1956, though, Deere deemed it necessary to change its logo yet again, almost certainly because of the company's increasing presence in industrial tractor and machinery markets. For the 1956 logo, Deere eliminated both the "ground" section used in the 1950 logo and the words "QUALITY FARM EQUIPMENT", which were located within it. Deere & Company definitely still produced quality farm equipment in 1956, but the company did far more than just that. Indeed, Deere had made huge strides in producing industrial tractors and equipment by that time. The new logo also looked more sleek, more modern, and more forceful than the 1950 trademark had. Deere's industrial equipment, in addition to its farm equipment, was also all of those things—more sleek, more modern, and certainly more advanced—in 1956.

The 1956 logo did a great job of still being current or up to date even with all the changes that took place in Deere's industrial production and marketing over the next several years.

This 1956 Deere trademark logo has seen lots of wear over the past 45 years. Still, the logo remains representative of the era when this tractor—a Model 840—was produced. And the tractor, mind you, still has a lot of hearty purr left in it despite its age.

participated in such a large public showing of industrial machines.

Deere greatly expanded upon the initial sales department that it had set up in 1956. According to Alm, Deere & Company "appointed" its first dealers for industrial equipment in either late 1957 or early 1958. (It is unclear when exactly Deere's agreement with Caterpillar regarding the marketing of Deere industrial tractors ended, but the agreement clearly had likely ceased by this time. Interestingly, prior to 1957, many John Deere dealers were also Caterpillar distributors. Starting around 1957, however, many of the combination Deere-Caterpillar dealers dropped the Caterpillar franchise. The seeming coincidence likely has much to do with Deere's new, improved industrial program.) The new John Deere dealership arrangement for selling industrial tractors consisted of dealers of two types: The industrial-carrying dealers were either industrial-only dealerships, or they sold both industrial and agricultural Deere products. Of course, Deere continued to authorize agricultural-only dealerships as well. Alm reports in his book that "each branch house was asked to designate someone to be responsible for industrial equipment sales."

The positive changes within Deere & Company didn't just mean a different way of doing business. Accompanying the company's increased emphasis on industrial production came two new model series that rocked the market. One of those came from

From the side, the Model 840 really doesn't resemble any typical tractor. And indeed, the 840 isn't typical — it's an industrial tractor. Made for brawny duty, the heavyweight's body was designed to withstand a beating; this one's has certainly stood the test of time.

The Model 440 came as either a wheel tractor or a crawler, although the crawler unit seems to be the most well known. This 440 crawler is hard at work loading logs. *Deere & Company Archives.*

Deere's Model 840 fitted with the Model 400 scraper, as seen here, had an impressive load capacity of 7 1/2 cubic yards. With scraper attached, the unit weighed in at over 23,000 pounds dry weight unloaded. *Randy Leffingwell*

Dubuque, while the other came from Waterloo.

Deere Unleashes Its 440 Series

For the 1958 model year, Deere & Company did far more for its industrial line than just introduce more industrial derivatives of agricultural tractors. Instead, for the first time, Deere & Company introduced a model that was strictly industrial. It had its own separate model designation—the 440 series—not just the same old

agricultural model designation supplemented by the letter "I."

Admittedly, the 440 series did branch off from one of Deere's agricultural tractor series, tracing its roots all the way back to the Model M of 1947, and the 440 tractors did share many things with the Model 430 and 435 John Deeres. For instance, the diesel versions of the 440—the 440ID wheel tractor and 440ICD crawler—used the same two-cylinder GM diesel engine that the 435 used. Similarly, the gasoline

versions of the 440—the 440I wheel tractor and 440IC crawler—used the same engine used in the 430 tractors. The 440 gassers could crank out more horsepower than the 430s could, however, due largely to the fact that Deere increased the rated rpm of the model to a full 2,000 turns a minute.

But the 440 wasn't the Model 430 or the Model 435. The 440 was a tractor all its own. It had a style and build quite unlike those of the agricultural models. For instance,

As the old saying urges, "Lead, follow, or get out of the way." The Model 840 Deere certainly led in many ways, and oftentimes, if anything dared get in its way, this brute could push it aside. In truth, the heavy front bumper on the 840 wasn't used for pushing that much, but it did provide protection for the unit's front end.

while the agricultural models featured sleek lines that easily caught one's attention, the 440 featured a different kind of sleek styling. The 440's styling was plainer and more functional than that of the agricultural models. And its design was more functional because it had to be. Industrial applications can be tough on tractors and their sheet metal, and the 440's sheet metal was designed to stand up to the test. For instance, the sleek side covers over the engine didn't just give the model an accurate appearance of grace and power; that sleek sheet metal also protected the engine from the elements and from the environment—whether it be rocks, lumber, or any other sort of material an industrial tractor might be working in or with—more so than did the agricultural models' sheet metal. The 440's design also made it harder for dirt to stick around, since there were fewer crevices for dirt to collect in.

The Model 440 was an appealing tractor for more reasons than its good looks and power. The 440 also made good marks when it came to the variety of jobs it could perform. These were made possible by coupling the unit with a variety of attachments. For instance, the 440 served as the first backhoe for John Deere. The 440 could be fitted with either the Model 50 backhoe, which mounted centrally on the back end of the tractor, or with the Model 51 backhoe, a unique backhoe that could be moved to the right or left of the center position on the back of the tractor to any of five different

A cab was offered as an option for the 840, a feature that gave operators a bit more protection. The cab also helped cut down on the amount of dirt swirling around the operator — pulling a scraper can be a hot, dirty job. *Randy Leffingwell*

positions. Furthermore, 440 owners could mate the tractor with the Model 71 loader (which had an optional crane attachment), the Model 24 scarifier, the rear-mounted Model 80 grading and finishing blade, the Model 301 angling bulldozer blade, or the Model 300

sideboom with optional pipe-bender attachment. Other items one could install on the 440 included a log loader, a fireline plow, a log arch, a winch, and even a trencher. Obviously, the 440 could fill many shoes and do many jobs, so it's no surprise that it impressed many people.

The Deere 840 Powers Up

The year 1958 proved itself important for Deere's heavy industrial equipment line. That year, in addition to introducing the Model 830 Industrial tractor as a supplement to the regular Model 830 agricultural tractor, Deere brought out

While many previous John Deere industrials came fitted with optional headlights, the 840 was one of the company's first tractors boasting that feature as standard equipment. Note how the headlights on this tractor are protected by the unit's heavy body.

yet another heavyweight industrial tractor based on the 830. Like the 830 Industrial, this new model—the Model 840—was commonly teamed up with a scraper. Indeed, even though not every 840 was fitted with a scraper, the 840 first started production as a tractor fitted with a Hancock scraper. That scraper was the same one used in conjunction with the Model 830-I, having a 7 1/2-cubic-yard capacity and measuring 8 feet wide by 7 feet, 8 inches tall when in transport position.

The Model 840 was similar to the 830 Industrial in many other ways. For instance, both models used the very same monster of an engine, with a 6 1/8x8-inch bore and stroke producing an impressive 471.5 cubic inches of displacement. Rated at 1,125 rpm with a heavy-handed 16:1 compression ratio, the engine could produce a rated 75.6 horsepower via the PTO; nearly 70 of those horses could find their way to the ground if needed. Furthermore, both the 830-I and the 840 used the same basic designs with regard to tractor chassis, hood, and grille. Both used the same huge 32.5-gallon fuel tank, a feature that allowed these highly efficient machines to work for hours on end without refueling. Both the 830-I

It takes a high-stepper to reach the 840's platform with just one step. Thankfully, Deere installed a simple yet very effective step just below the platform to help in that regard. Note also the mesh material located on the tractor's floorboard, a material that cut down significantly on the possibility of an operator slipping on the platform.

left: In the driver's seat, the operator of an 840 enjoys easy-to-reach controls and easy-to-see gauges such as these. These gauges are on the top of the tractor's hood, which is located directly to the right of the operator's position.

below: In terms of direct line of descent, the Model 840 could perhaps be considered the ultimate industrial descendant of the Model R, the initial model which helped put Deere on the heavy industrial equipment map. The 840 would soon yield to an even more advanced model, the Model 5010 industrial.

Perhaps the hardest to reach of the 840's basic controls is its gearshift. Note the bends in this model's gearshift lever, bends that made it possible for the operator to select gears without Deere having to entirely redesign or reposition the tractor's transmission.

and the 840 could be ordered using either a split-load 24-12-volt electric start system or a V-4 gasoline-starting engine. That's just about where the similarity between these two models ended, however.

Indeed, the 840 had many characteristics that make it instantly distinguishable from the 830-I. For instance, the operator's platform on the 840 was not behind the hood and fuel tank as it is on the 830-I or

most of the other John Deere tractors then in production. Instead, that station was located on the left side of the hood and engine of the tractor, midway between the front and rear wheels. Consequently, all of the operator controls on the 840 were arranged differently. Furthermore, the Model 840 used an overall sheet metal style very similar to that used on the Model 440. Thus, like its little brother, the 840's

appearance screamed brute power but still emitted an essence of grace. Like the 440, the 840's style made it functional in a very eye-appealing sort of way.

Deere fitted the 840 with special heavy-duty fenders that extended from the front of the tractor clear to the back. The only other tractor ever previously built that had fenders that looked anything even remotely similar to the 840's was

From the back, just as from the front, the Model 840 is obviously a "whole lotta" tractor! The heavyweight machine was well designed to pull heavy equipment—scrapers in particular. Note the two mounts for the scraper located inside each fender below the level of the SMV sign on this unit.

the Model UDLX Comfortractor, which the Minneapolis-Moline Power Implement Company built way back in 1938. But the UDLX's fenders were designed the way they were for stylistic, aesthetic reasons. The 840 John Deere's fenders had a practical design purpose: they helped protect the tractor as well as the operator. They didn't just extend from the rear of the tractor to the front—they reached from near the top of the tractor's hood all the way down to the bottom of the tractor's chassis. Thus, the operator's station was located *in* the left-hand fender assembly, while the right-hand fender entirely covered up the tractor's clutch pulley. That wasn't a problem, though, since the 840 wasn't intended for any jobs that would require the use of an endless belt powered off the clutch pulley and connected to some remote piece of equipment. The main drawback with the full-cover fenders of this model, though, was that it made access to engine components somewhat more challenging.

Another difference between the 830-I and the 840 was the tire equipment. For instance, the 840 came with 8-26 ten-ply rear tires, which had been optional on the 830-I. Furthermore, the 840 featured

The industrial John Deere 5010 — a derivative of Deere's new Model 5010 tractor in the New Generation of Power series — took over the reign of being the heavy-duty industrial wheel tractor in Deere's line. Supplanting the Model 840, the 5010 also saw use as a scraper unit as seen here. *Deere & Company Archives*

larger front tires than the 830-I used, coming standard with 8.25x20 ten-ply front tires. Deere made 11.00x16 eight-ply flotation-type tires available for the 840 as well. The 840 also had different forward speeds than the standard 830: while the 830 had a forward speed range from 2 1/3 miles per hour to 12 3/4 miles per hour, the 840 had slower forward

speeds, ranging from 1 3/4 miles per hour to 11 1/4 miles per hour. And whereas the 830 had a reverse speed of 2 3/4 miles per hour, the 840 had a slower reverse of only 2 1/4 miles per hour.

For the 1958 model year, a total of 63 Model 840 tractors were assembled. Deere then sent all of those basic tractors to Lubbock,

Texas, where the Hancock Manu-facturing Company fitted their scrapers and made all necessary changes. Things changed for the 1959 model year, however. At that time, Deere decided to add the scrapers to the tractors at its Water-loo, Iowa, factory. These Deere-assembled tractor-scraper units (which became known as "New

Like many Deere machines throughout history, the JD440 log skidder was available with different accessories. This unit, for example, features a log grapple attachment. Note the rear-mounted operator station for operating that tool. *Deere & Company Archives*

Style 840s") featured a few improvements over the 1958 versions, and Deere wanted to offer owners of the 1958 models the opportunity to benefit from those conversions. Many customers requested to have their 1958 model 840s brought up to "New Style" standards. Deere also decided that it would give 820 owners who had had Hancock scrapers installed on their tractors the opportunity to update their tractors as well. As a result, seven

Model 820 tractors received what Deere & Company referred to in its records as an "entire modification." Those tractors included 820s numbered 8205287, 8205288, 8205686, 8205697, 8205698, 8205782, 8205783, and 8205890. (Note: It is entirely possible that 840 number 8400026 either did not initially receive a Hancock scraper, or, if it did, was not updated to "New Style" standards as discussed later; that tractor is not listed in Deere documents

indicating which 820s received the scrapers. All other 840s from serial number 8400000 to 8400062 are accounted for in those documents.)

Early in the 1960 model year, Deere made further changes to the 840 tractor-scraper combinations. Instead of adding Hancock scrapers, Deere & Company started installing its own Model 400 elevating scraper onto the 840s. That practice continued until the end of 840 production.

Deere dropped its Model 840 from its line one full year after discontinuing the Models 830 and 830 Industrial. Those two models officially terminated on June 1, 1961, while the 840 officially terminated on June 1, 1962. Deere's Decision D25950 of March 3, 1961, listed the termination dates for all three of those models as well as other agricultural tractors in Deere's line.

Establishment of the John Deere Industrial Equipment Works

Late in 1958, Deere & Company did even more to establish the permanency of its industrial tractor and machinery production. In a company Bulletin dated November 26, 1958, Deere & Company Vice President George T. French announced that the John Deere Wagon Works was being renamed—the new name would be the "John Deere Industrial Equipment Works." According to French, the name change would take place on December 1, 1958. The company had been actively involved in shifting the focus of production of the Wagon Works from agricultural implements to industrial units. Thus, in his Bulletin, French stated "this factory and its management organization will eventually be devoted entirely to the design, development, manufacture, and promotion of industrial equipment products, and this new name will be appropriate to the objectives of the organization." So starting on December 1, 1958, not only did Deere have an entire division devoted to industrial products, it had an entire factory for that purpose as well.

The Early New Generation Industrial Tractors

August 30, 1960, otherwise known as Deere Day, marked the introduction of Deere's new "New Generation of Power." That day in Dallas, Texas, Deere & Company unveiled the new model series, complete with something many people thought they'd never see in a John Deere tractor: four- and six-cylinder engines. Included in the lineup were the Models 1010, 2010, 3010, and 4010. Those agricultural tractor models took center stage in Dallas that day, and they would be the foundation for Deere's new line of industrial tractors.

For a time, the industrial versions of the New Generation tractors were almost identical to their agricultural counterparts with the addition of some heavier components, particularly in the area of sheet metal. And, as one would expect, the industrial New Generation tractors typically received a yellow paint job. The industrial tractors also featured heavier frame rails and front axles as a general rule.

The first few models of New Generation industrial tractors included the Model 1010 in both wheel tractor and crawler configurations, the Model 2010 in both wheel tractor and crawler configurations, and the 3010 and 4010 wheel tractors. Of all the New Generation industrials, the 1010 crawler had perhaps the most interesting story. It, like the 440 that it supplanted, could come fitted with a variety of attachments. They included a loader, backhoe, the Model 612 dozer blade controlled by Deere's "T-bar" control system, the Model 600 brush and rock rake, and two other bulldozer blade models, the 610 and the 624. The 1010 crawlers fitted with either the 610 or 624 dozer blades and could also be fitted with Deere's Model 340 rotoboom on the back of the unit. For those 1010 crawlers that did not have the dozer blades, a special high-lift log loader could also be used.

In 1963, Deere brought out yet another new industrial model based on the New Generation tractor series. The new model, the Model 5010-I, came out as the replacement for the 840. Like the 840, the 5010-I usually came fitted with a scraper. The 5010-I featured a big 531-ci six-cylinder engine with a bore and stroke of 4.75x5 inches. The big tractor, which weighed in at over 13,500 pounds, produced roughly 129 horsepower. According to advertising literature for the model, it's advanced transmission provided eight forward speeds ranging from 2.6 to 26.11 miles per hour, plus three reverse speeds ranging from 5.3 to 14.2 miles per hour. The model came standard with power steering, key ignition, tachometer, fuel gauge, ammeter, hour meter, horn, cigarette lighter, and much more.

New Industrial Models for 1964

For the 1964 model year, the New Generation 3010 and 4010 industrial tractors stepped aside to

DID YOU KNOW?
RUMORS OF FOUR-CYLINDER ENGINES

Dozens of years before Deere introduced its New Generation tractors in 1960, rumors abounded in the tractor industry that Deere was soon going to introduce four-cylinder engines in its tractors. Many people thought those claims were absurd, thinking that Deere would never get rid of its well-known two-cylinder engine design. But some people actually did believe—or at least had some suspicions—that Deere might go to four cylinders.

Why would anyone believe such a thing? There are many possibilities. For instance, many people had criticized Deere in the past for sticking to its two-cylinder design. Those opponents of the design claimed that the two-cylinder engine didn't deliver power evenly, and many were convinced—even without in-depth knowledge as to how and why Deere's two-cylinder design actually *was* an effective design—that four-cylinder engines had to be more powerful simply because they had more cylinders. Other people thought it possible that Deere might go to the four-cylinder engines because they felt that the two-cylinder engine couldn't get much more powerful than the level it was already at, even back in the 1930s.

When Deere got word of those early rumors that it was working on a four-cylinder engine, the company emphatically denied them. Deere & Company was devoted to its two-cylinder engine design; it was efficient, it delivered the power needed, and it had a simple design. The latter was a big factor for two reasons: First, many farmers at the time chose to work on their own machines, and the simpler the design, the better they liked it. Second, a two-cylinder engine required roughly half the parts needed in a four-cylinder engine, and that meant fewer things in Deere's two-cylinder engine that could eventually wear out.

With time, almost everyone came to realize that Deere was, indeed, very dedicated to its two-cylinder engines. And many eventually understood why. Furthermore, Deere proved it possible to make two-cylinder engines far more powerful. Bigger bores weren't the only answer. Longer strokes and higher compression ratios and higher-rated engine speeds helped increase power tremendously. Furthermore, Deere's engineers figured out ways to make fuel burn more cleanly and efficiently by making changes to cylinder heads and piston tops—in essence, changing the atmosphere of the combustion chamber.

Deere's actions did prove that the company was not afraid of experimenting with engines, but it became evident to many that Deere seemed to insist that those engines always be of two-cylinder design. For example, Deere introduced a new upright engine in 1938 with the Model L that was still a two-cylinder. Deere apparently liked the upright two-cylinder design so well that the company continued to use its basic concepts in models such as the M, the 40, 420, and even the new 320. All those tractors used two-cylinder engines. And when Deere introduced a revolutionary, highly efficient and effective diesel engine in the 1949 Model R, it was still a two-cylinder. It seemed the two-cylinder engine was in Deere's line to stay. The rumors of four-cylinder engines in John Deere tractors subsided. Then in 1960, Deere surprised the world, when the dead rumors became living realities.

be replaced by the Model 500 and 600 industrial tractors, respectively.

A Broader Line in 1965

In 1965, Deere & Company set the tone for the near future of its industrial tractor production. Deere came out with several new models that would serve as the beginnings of Deere's major moves to expand its industrial offerings. At the same time, Deere started using a new model designation system that set its industrial machines entirely apart from the agricultural models. The new model designation system for John Deere industrials consisted of the letters "JD," followed immediately by a three-digit number that would have a specific meaning. If any major updates or changes were made to those models, Deere would simply amend the model designation by adding a dash and a letter. In most cases, the amended letter would start with "A" or "B" then be replaced by the next letter in the alphabet if more improvements were made later, and so forth.

The JD440 Log Skidder

The Model JD440 log skidder served as the first machine built by Deere specifically for the purpose of skidding logs in the forestry industry. The JD440 skidder featured an articulated frame and four-wheel-drive power.

The JD480 Forklift

The first true forklift in Deere's line, the JD480, wasn't just a forklift

The New Generation series did much to change the face not only of Deere's agricultural tractors but also its industrial line. The effects of that revolution in thinking and styling can still be seen, for instance, on this Model JD480-B forklift.

attachment put on the back of a converted tractor. A unit in and of itself, the JD480 featured either a 180-ci gasoline engine or a 202-ci diesel engine. The model featured eight forward and eight reverse speeds and hydrostatic power steering, and customers could order the unit with either a 14- or 21-foot mast. The JD480 could handle up to 5,000 pounds in vertical lift up to 14 feet high on either mast, but the most that the 21-foot mast could lift to its full height was 2,500 pounds. Overall, the JD480 was a great start in the fork-lift market, and it set the tone for future Deere forklifts.

New Wheel Tractors and Crawlers

Just as the Model 3010 and 4010 industrials had been replaced by the 400 and 500 in 1964, the John Deere 1010 and 2010 series indus-trials stepped aside to make way for the JD300 and JD400 tractors of 1966. These industrial trac-tors were available in both wheel tractor type and crawler tractor form, like their predecessors.

The JD350 and JD450 Crawlers: Either Bulldozers or Crawler Loaders, Your Choice

In 1965, Deere & Company intro-duced two new crawler models to replace the 1010 and 2010 crawlers. The new models—the JD350 and JD450—could be fitted with either a dozer blade or a loader bucket, thus converting the crawlers into full-fledged bulldozers or crawler loaders.

The JD480 and its descendants certainly had impressive lifting capabilities. The original model was available with either a 14-foot or a 21-foot mast, which provided respective corresponding lift heights. Some of the JD480's progeny, including the JD480-B with 21-foot mast seen here, had similar options.

CHAPTER 6

Expanding the Industrial Line

By the mid- to late 1960s, Deere & Company's Industrial Division had become a well-established, well-respected part of the company. The line included wheeled general-use tractors, scrapers, crawlers and bulldozers, and log skidders, among other things. In addition to those Deere-built machines, John Deere industrials could be coupled with many different pieces of related equipment produced by other manufacturers.

By the mid- to late-1960s, Deere had a very firm footing in the industrial market. Its products had proven themselves not only effective but also reliable and efficient. The company was ready to do more, to produce more on its own. In that manner, Deere wouldn't have to rely on other manufacturers to make attachments that would work on John Deere industrials. So in the late 1960s, Deere started to fill in almost every gap that existed in the company's industrial line.

One of the gaps that Deere & Company identified was road graders. Deere's products had a history of making and maintaining roads, and its scrapers did much to help in that category. But Deere recognized that it lacked a true road grader, despite the fact that road graders had appeared quite a bit earlier in the company's history.

Perhaps the earliest John Deere tractors used as road graders were Model D industrial tractors. Initially, Deere had teamed up with Caterpillar to have industrial versions of the John Deere Model D pull that company's pull-type road graders. Not long after that, the D was fitted with the Hawkeye road maintainer. Those Model D Hawkeye Motor Patrol tractors looked very much like today's road graders, but their production was quite limited. Following the Hawkeye road maintainer experiment, Deere didn't do much to convert its industrial tractors into road graders. The

Deere & Company's Industrial Division just kept growing from the 1960s on. With a solid industrial market foundation to build upon, Deere soon added a variety of new industrial machines that could do even more jobs. Among those items introduced were Deere's ever-so-versatile skid steer loaders.

John Deere's Model JD570 motor grader was certainly a revolutionary machine. It filled a gap in Deere's industrial lineup that had existed for years, and its articulated frame proved that Deere still meant business in the motor grader market. *Deere & Company Archives*

Like so many other John Deere products, the JD544 loader could come with a number of special features and attachments. Note that this unit features a backhoe attachment, making it in effect a backhoe loader. *Deere & Company Archives*

company's tractors still were excellent units with which to pull trailing-type, nonpowered graders, but by the mid-1960s, Deere decided it wanted to do more.

Filling the Grader Gap: The Model JD570 Motor Grader

Deere entered the motor grader market in 1968 with its John Deere Model JD570. This was a regular production road grader produced entirely by Deere & Company. As important as that might be, though, it wasn't the most significant thing about the JD570 grader. Deere documents indicate that the JD570 motor grader entered the market as the first motor grader that featured steering via an articulating frame. That steering system came *in addition to* the usual front-wheel steering system that most road graders had featured up until that time.

Loaders often feature articulated frames, which give them shorter turning radii. These big machines sometimes work in close quarters (such as between piles of rock or other such material), so the quicker they can turn, the easier it is to get them wherever they are needed.

DID YOU KNOW?
SOME PRINCIPLES OF ROAD GRADER OPERATION

Most companies or governments use road graders exactly for what the machines' names imply—grading roads. This task initially looks like nothing more than pushing dirt around. And indeed, that usually happens when a road grader is at work. But in order to grade a road as smooth as it can be, a road grader operator can't just drop the grader's blade abruptly and start pushing dirt any way he or she wishes. That approach would produce a modest but still noticeable bump in the road. The section immediately behind the blade at that starting point would be higher than the section moved with the lowered blade. To avoid that problem, the blade should in ideal circumstances be dropped *gradually*, or—as grader operators say—the blade needs to be "feathered in." Hydraulic controls to some degree help feather in the blade, as the operator can lower the blade little by little until it reaches the desired depth of cut in the road.

While gradually increasing the cut in the road by feathering in the blade in small yet steady increments is very important, the reverse principle is even more important at the end of the stretch being

Another advantage in having the grader blade located toward the center of the machine is that the operator can clearly see most of the blade in that position and more quickly determine whether to make any changes in the blade's positioning or angling.

graded. If the operator simply left the blade at the same cut depth throughout the entire grading period, the blade would accumulate a lot of dirt and rock in front of it. Promptly raising the blade would then deposit this material as a big hump in the road surface. To avoid leaving such a hump, the grader operator must gradually lift the blade when nearing the end of the stretch being graded. Again, hydraulic controls make that task easier to perform.

To make a smooth road that drains properly, the operator of a road grader

has to make sure that the blade is set at all the right angles. In all, there are three blade angles a road grader operator must consider when grading a road: One angle, in which one end of the blade is located farther forward than the other end, is important in determining how much dirt is moved across the blade, and how quickly. Another angle—the horizontal positioning of the blade, where one end of the blade is often higher than the other end—is important in determining how much of a crown a road has. The crown, or raised center portion of the road, allows water to drain into side ditches rather than pool on the road surface. The final blade angle—in which the top of the blade is located either farther forward, directly over, or farther behind the bottom of the blade—determines how well packed the dirt of the road is after being graded. All those blade angles can easily be controlled by hydraulics.

While operators often rely on hydraulic controls for the subtle blade movements necessary to produce a smooth road with a proper crown, they rely as much on the articulated frame for another road-grading task—pulling up ditches. To drain properly, roads must be built up above the height of the

The profile of almost any motor grader looks almost the same from unit to unit, a fact that shows that the general design on those units is both tried and true. The grader's mid-mounted blade helps to keep the graded area more level—with fewer humps and bumps—than front- or rear-mounted blades can accomplish.

Sometimes when the going gets tough for a grader — or rather, the ground gets tough — the operator can drop the rippers to break up the surface being graded. This makes more dirt available, from deeper depths.

surrounding ground. This is done with dirt taken from ditches constructed on either side, into which water drains from rain or melting snow. With repeated grading, however, the road surface falls and the ditches take in the extra dirt. Then, to restore proper road height and drainage, the ditches must be "pulled up"—grader operators reclaim dirt from the ditches and use it to build up the road. An articulated frame makes it much easier for grader and operator to perform this task.

If the ditch being pulled up involves uneven or unstable ground, the articulated frame can be adjusted so that the right front wheel of the grader runs in the ditch while the rear drive wheels remain on the more even or stable road surface. This approach isn't foolproof: sometimes it causes directional difficulties, driving the grader toward the ditch—but it can help in some situations.

The articulated frame can also help a grader operator steer around the windrow of dirt left by the blade from a prior pass in the opposite direction. Avoiding the windrow helps keep the tractor and blade from bouncing up and down and producing ridges in the road known as "rub boards" or "washboards."

Obviously, hydraulics and an articulated frame were important things in motor grader development. The JD570 had both, and it was the first road grader produced with the latter.

Even when the skies turn dark with rain rolling in, this John Deere loader stands ready to get to work, just as its ancestors from decades before did. This unit, a Model 444H, descended from the original Model JD440 loader and its progeny.

Why was an articulating road grader such a big deal? The most obvious advantage was that the feature gave the JD570 a shorter turning radius than it would have had with a fixed frame. More important, though, the articulated frame allowed operators to position the grader in ways that were extremely advantageous to road building and maintenance.

The JD570 grader also was heir to a technology first introduced in Deere products with the Model R tractor some 19 years earlier. The JD570 was the first John Deere grader powered by a diesel engine. This diesel engine could produce around 83 horsepower, sufficient for most jobs a road grader would be called on to tackle. Deere also equipped the JD570 with a differential lock, which helped reduce drive-wheel slippage and skidding in turns or under load (that feature could to some degree compensate for the problems discussed in pulling up ditches with the frame articulated). The JD570's front wheels could also lean up to 20 degrees from vertical, a feature that made operating on the slight lean of a road when grading (from the crown down to the ditches), or on the drastic lean when pulling up ditches, more feasible.

The Model JD544 Loader Lines Up

Deere & Company also recognized that it didn't have a true loader tractor in its lineup, either. The company had had many different tractor models that could be

DEERE TRADEMARK LOGO CORNER:
A LASTING CHANGE IN 1968

By 1968, Deere had made tremendous gains in marketing its industrial tractors and other machines, and the John Deere name was becoming well known on construction sites and in forestry operations in many different places on earth. With the company's growing presence in industrial markets and its continued improvements and innovations in a host of other markets—including, for example, agricultural and residential grounds care markets, among others—Deere & Company changed its trademark logo yet again. This time, the new logo bore a close resemblance to the one it replaced, but there were some distinct differences. For instance, the leaping deer emblem no longer showed four legs as all previous versions had. Instead, the 1968 logo gave more of a profilelike image of the deer, with only one back leg and one front leg showing in the logo. Aside from that and other changes that were made to the deer, the only other noticeable changes included the use of a different text style for the name "JOHN DEERE" (which was still located beneath the deer) and the curved edges of the logo were a little flatter than they had been in the 1956 version. The overall border of the new logo was closer to being square-shaped, too, although it still was wider than it was tall.

The logo Deere introduced in 1968 would stay around for a long time, and some people may have thought it would become permanent. But eventually, Deere saw yet another need for a change in logo. The company kept moving forward as it always has.

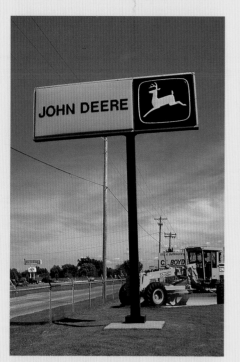

This John Deere industrial dealer's sign still bears the old logo introduced in 1968. It is not unusual to see this older logo, as the new one was just introduced in 2000 and some dealers haven't yet been able to update their signs.

This stool in a local John Deere dealership shows the progression of Deere & Company's trademark logo from 1837 up until the 1968 logo, which stayed current for approximately 30 years. Note how all of the leaping deer in these logos are landing, whereas the deer in the most recent logo (introduced in 2000) is starting to jump.

fitted with aftermarket loaders, but never before had the company produced a machine that was specifically a loader unit by itself. Some jobs for which a loader was needed were much too demanding on the small-capacity tractor-attached loader buckets. The company decided to build a true loader with a bucket large enough to handle those bigger jobs much more efficiently.

In 1968, Deere filled the loader gap by releasing the Model JD544 hydraulic front-end loader unit. This loader traced its roots back to the Model 440 John Deere. Deere had converted the 440 into a four-wheel-drive articulated log skidder for forestry work back in 1965. The next year, Deere released the improved 440A log skidder, and then in 1968 it introduced the brand-new JD540 log skidder to replace it. The JD540 log skidder and the JD544 loader used essentially the same basic chassis design, the principal difference being that the loader featured a hydraulic front-end loader/bucket while the log skidder featured the logging apparatus. Note that, with the introduction of the JD544 loader, Deere started using the numbers "44" as the last two digits in the three-digit model number to indicate that the unit was a four-wheel-drive loader. From that point forward, Deere also used "40" as the last two digits in the model designation number for log skidders.

Available with either a gasoline or diesel engine, the JD544 loader was a big machine with big power.

It touted an impressive 94 horsepower, and with that oomph it could handle big loads.

Like its predecessors, the JD544 also featured articulated steering. Four-wheel drive power gave the loader the added traction needed in tough terrain. Deere made a version of the JD544 available with a special loader intended for use in loading logs.

For the year 1969, Deere released yet another hydraulic loader—the Model JD644. Even bigger than the JD544, the new model could handle loads up to 12,500 pounds with its increased horsepower. The JD644

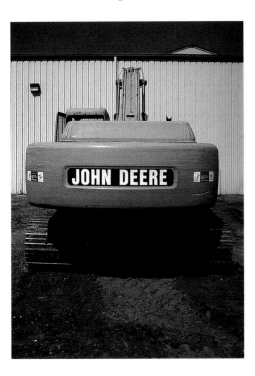

For many years, Deere & Company labeled its industrials with large letters distinguishing the name "JOHN DEERE", as seen on the back of this excavator. More recent John Deere industrials, however, feature noticeably different labeling. Later machines simply bear the word "DEERE". The name is instantly, easily recognizable, almost as if to say "Deere: Enough Said."

John Deere started producing large hydraulic excavators back in 1969 with the Model JD690, one of the predecessors to this more modern unit.

The 310 series John Deere backhoe loaders first appeared approximately 30 years ago, and the series still exists today. The modern 310 series, though, features many improvements over its ancestors, as well as amended model designations.

could produce around 131 horsepower with either a gasoline or diesel engine. Like the JD544, the JD644 could also be made specifically into a log loader unit.

New Backhoe Loaders Hit the Market: Enter the JD310, JD410, JD510, and JD500-C

For the 1971 model year, Deere unveiled four new backhoe loaders models. They included the 50-horsepower Model JD310, the 62-horsepower Model JD410, the 80-horsepower Model JD510, and the similarly powered Model JD500-C backhoe loaders. The

JD310 and JD410 both featured reverser transmissions, the JD310 having eight forward and four reverse speeds, and the JD410 having eight speeds in both directions. The JD510 and JD500-C backhoe loaders both had Deere's "Power Shift" transmissions with eight forward and four reverse speeds, and those two models were available with diesel-powered engines only.

As important as the engine and transmission features of all four of these models were, those things perhaps weren't the most important aspects of the newly introduced machines. Deere documents

indicate that those four new models—the JD310, JD410, JD510, and JD500-C—were the first backhoe loaders in the industry that featured closed-center hydraulics. That feature would soon become an industry standard in agricultural and industrial tractors alike.

Two New Utility Models for 1971: The JD301 and JD401

Paralleling Deere's introduction of the JD310 and JD410 backhoe loaders was Deere's introduction of two utility tractors with similar designations, the JD301 and JD401 tractors. Both models employed

John Deere's move into the skid steer market came in the 1970s with the JD14 and JD24 skid steer models. Small units, these machines could perform in much closer quarters than the much larger four-wheel-drive loaders or other industrial machines. *Deere & Company Archives*

This more modern John Deere skid steer loader shows how much the machines have evolved over time, but it's also evident that the basic design is nearly the same as that used on the earliest skid steers. Today's machines, however, feature many improvements over their predecessors, including better lift systems, for instance.

While some skid steers can be fitted with a forklift attachment, they usually can't lift things to nearly the same height that a true forklift unit can. Skid steers often prove more versatile than forklifts for a variety of reasons, however.

reverser transmissions and featured power steering, two-speed live PTOs, and rockshafts with three-point hitches. The JD301 had a net horsepower rating of 43, whereas the JD401 rated 59 horsepower in the same category.

The Skid Steers Come on the Scene

By the 1970s, Deere & Company had noticed that there was a relatively new product on the industrial market that had strong potential to be a hot seller. It was perhaps the smallest thing ever to come onto the industrial scene, but—as the old saying goes—big things sometimes come in small packages. And for John Deere, skid steer loaders became a very big thing despite their small, compact size.

Deere introduced its first skid steer loader—the Model JD24—in 1970, and the company's timing in entering this market was excellent. Skid steers were starting to become fairly popular both in factories and on construction sites, and their popularity would only rise in the years to come. The first skid steers appeared on the market around 1960, introduced by Bobcat.

Five years after releasing the JD24, Deere came out with yet another skid steer. But this time it

As Deere kept introducing new kinds of industrial machines, the company also kept making improvements to its other machines in production. According to Brian R. Alm's book, prior to about 1980, whenever Deere updated such models extensively, the company placed a dash after the model series number followed by a letter from the alphabet. "A" was often the first such letter used, to be replaced by "B," to be replaced by "C," and so on.

was even smaller. Designated the Model JD14, the new model proved quite popular on a variety of construction sites. The two models—the JD14 and the JD24—would set the stage for future John Deere skid steer loader production, and in true John Deere fashion, Deere & Company found a variety of new and innovative ways to make those machines all the more reliable, versatile, and popular.

Deere's ERA III of 1974

When looking back on the history of John Deere industrial production, a number of years stand out among the rest as pivotal years. They include 1936, 1949, 1956, 1957, and 1958. But one would be remiss to leave the year 1974 out of that list. Deere's industrial production had come a long way by that time, but things were only just beginning. The year 1974

was to be the start of a new era in Deere industrial history, and for a couple of reasons.

Deere officials, in fact, formally declared the year a new era. According to Brian R. Alm's *A History of the John Deere Industrial Equipment Division*, Deere started what it called "ERA III." Alm writes that ERA III was a program that "proposed to introduce a number of larger construction and

forestry machines between 1975 and 1979." Alm goes on to indicate that those machines would include "a 90,000-pound excavator, four more motor graders, a large four-wheel-drive loader, an improved scraper, and four crawlers with hydrostatic drive transmissions." As quoted in Alm's book, Mr. Delno W. Brown —then senior vice president in charge of industrial equipment operations, component sales, foundry operations, and outside manufactured products for both the United States and Canada—stated, "The name ERA III helps to signify how important the next few years will be. It sets them apart from ERA I, the years of our industrial beginnings, and from ERA II, our developing years in the 1960s and early 1970s." Obviously, Deere had big plans for its future.

Davenport Works Starts Production

The other big thing that happened in 1974 (and was possibly in part the result of the goals of ERA III) was the establishment of Deere's Davenport Works. Production of industrial equipment began at that facility in December of 1974 and continues there today. Products produced there include motor graders, log skidders, four-wheel-drive loaders, and more.

Alm's book also indicates that, starting around 1980, Deere & Company initiated a new practice for designating its industrial machines. At that time, Deere dropped the "JD" from the front of all of its industrials' designations. It also eliminated the hyphen between the base model series number and the amended letter on improved models.

More Motor Grader Innovations

In 1978, just 11 years after Deere turned heads with its JD570's articulated frame and other special

Deere & Company re-entered the motor grader market back in 1967 by introducing an innovative new model with special new features. Since that time, the company has continued to make many other improvements to its motor grader design.

features, Deere & Company again captured the spotlight. For the 1978 model year, Deere introduced its new JD672A and JD772A graders. These were the first graders with a unique front-wheel drive system that helped supply the grader with constant power. A system of sensors on the rear wheels instantly detected slippage and sent a signal to the hydrostatically powered front wheels to make their drive system engage automatically. This system is still used in some form on certain John Deere motor grader models.

An Impressive Lineup

Deere's industrial lineup by the mid-1960s was already impressive, but by the late 1970s it was even more so. In fact, Deere & Company's industrial line had grown so much that anyone would be hard-pressed to find many industrial jobs that Deere's machines couldn't handle. The company had everything from small, highly maneuverable skid steer loaders to large earthmoving excavators, and almost everything in between. And, with the list of options available for Deere

industrials, many of them could be made to do far more jobs than one might initially realize. Thus, with such a long line of equipment with so many different attachment options, John Deere industrials quickly found their way onto thousands of work sites in all sorts of places, ranging from giant metropolises to dense forests and everywhere else in between. And since Deere industrials proved highly reliable machines, they found their way into the hearts of a multitude of construction and forestry equipment owners and operators.

CHAPTER 7

Recent John Deere Industrials: A Full Line

Identifying every industrial tractor or model of construction or forestry machine in Deere & Company's line is now a daunting task. As Deere stays on the cutting edge, equipment within the lineup has to change to stay ahead of the times. New models appear quickly, further expanding the already-full line of quality industrial John Deere machines.

Defining what is recent is a subjective task. Because of their rugged construction, Deere machines from the 1980s, 1970s, and even earlier are still seeing regular use. For the purposes of this book, "recent" is defined as anything produced from the mid-1980s onward. There is not room to cover every model produced during that time, but the most noticeable machines in most (if not all) of the most noticeable categories will be addressed. For simplicity's sake, these machines will be discussed in categories, not in chronological order by date of introduction overall.

Backhoe Loaders: Extremely Versatile Machines

Today, backhoe loaders are among the most popular machines used for industrial work, whether by contractors, city and state governments, utility companies, or almost any other group that needs a multi-purpose machine. The key to a backhoe loader's versatility is its design.

Some people call backhoe loaders simply backhoes, but that description is a little narrow to convey the machine's full potential. Backhoe loaders consist of a tractor—nowadays usually cabbed—fitted with a loader on the front end and a backhoe arm on the back. Backhoes typically use the steering system of the tractor itself to maneuver from location to location and in direct conjunction with the use of the loader.

The components of a backhoe loader work well together, making the machine more than the sum of its components. Like any regular front-end loader, the

Today industrial John Deeres can be seen almost anywhere on land doing almost anything. And yes, some yellow-painted Deeres such as this one can still be found mowing roadsides, which was the primary duty performed by many of Deere's earliest industrial tractors. Present John Deere industrials can be used for so many more different types of applications than their early predecessors could, though.

This Model 310SG backhoe loader features front-wheel assist, whereas the one in the previous photo does not. Some backhoe loaders might need that extra bit of traction and pull, though, especially when working in loose or muddy soil.

Hydraulics play a major role on most Deere & Company industrial machines. They are used for a wide array of different tasks. Backhoe loaders, for instance, use hydraulics almost literally from the front of the unit all the way to the back.

unit's loader can be used for a variety of different jobs, like moving dirt, rock, wood chips, or other such loose material. This might involve merely transplanting those materials to a different location, loading those things into the backs of dump trucks, or using them for filling in holes. In the latter case, the loader bucket can be used to some degree to compact materials into such holes and also to smooth them over. But it's much easier for a loader to manipulate such materials if those materials are loose, and it's even better if they are in loose piles. That's where the backhoe component of a backhoe loader can help.

By itself, a backhoe is usually used for digging holes. Sometimes, if absolutely necessary, the bucket of a backhoe can be used not only to dig holes but also to move earth or other materials from a pile into a hole. It's much more efficient, however, to do that job with a loader. So, let's say that someone needs to dig down to repair a broken water main, for instance. A backhoe loader can be backed up to the location needed to be dug out, and can dig down to the appropriate depth so that the main can be repaired. (Sometimes it's best to have the backhoe dig down to close to the main, then have the remaining

Since signing on the expertise of Henry Dreyfuss & Associates way back in the 1930s, Deere & Company has made tremendous improvements in operator comfort and conveniences on its products. Today's machines not only have comfortable seats, but they also have easy-to-understand, easy-to-reach, easy-to-see, and easy-to-operate controls. Deere machines also give operators a superb view of the job at hand, whether it be in front of, alongside, or even behind the machine.

dirt removed with more sensitive tools—shovels, for instance.) Then, when everything has been fixed, the backhoe loader can turn around and use its loader to fill in the hole that the backhoe dug. This process is called backfilling, and it's one of the most important

things that makes backhoe loaders so popular and useful.

Today, Deere & Company offers a long line of backhoe loaders. These include the popular G series models, such as the 310G, 310SG, and the 410G—all of which trace their roots back to

the original Models 310 and 410 that came out in the early 1970s. But today, the 310 and 410 backhoes are greatly improved even over their respectable predecessors. For instance, according to Deere documents, the 310G with its four-cylinder 276-ci naturally aspirated engine produces 74 net horsepower while operating at 2,200 rpm. The 310SG (which features a turbocharged engine of the same size as the 310G's) is advertised at 84 net horsepower. Compare those numbers to the original Model JD310 backhoe, which only produced around 50 horsepower. Similarly, the John Deere 410G backhoe loader of today has an advertised net SAE horsepower of 92 at 2,000 rpm, while the original Model JD410 backhoe loader cranked out about 62 horsepower. Other current John Deere backhoe loaders are the Model 315G and the Model 710D, the latter being the stoutest such unit in Deere's current line. The 710D features a six-cylinder, 414-ci, turbocharged engine that produces an advertised 115 SAE net horsepower at 2,200 rpm. When fitted with the standard-equipment backhoe, the 710D has an advertised maximum digging depth of 18 feet, 2 inches, but when fitted with the optional extendable dipper stick, the 710D can dig as deep as 23 feet, 1 inch.

Loaders: From Factories to Forests and Many Places in Between

Deere & Company has produced a number of different versions of loaders and log loaders within the past several years, and today is no exception. The current lineup offers so many different styles and so many different features with so many different attachments that it's nearly impossible to know where to

When the support arms are lowered to the ground, they help eliminate tires "giving" under load. Support arms can have various kinds of "feet" or "pads" for use in different conditions. Two predominant types are rubber pads and the more traditional steel pads with some sort of cleats or ribbing.

Buckets aren't the only things that a person can attach to the backhoe arms of Deere's backhoe loaders. Another useful attachment, called a hammer or breaker (otherwise known as a jackhammer), can be used to break up pavement and is attached to the end of the backhoe arm.

start. Consider, for example, Deere's 744H series four-wheel-drive loaders. Those machines—which in 2001 came in three different base model variations, the 744H log loader, the 744H high-lift loader, and the 744H MH material handler—all featured Deere's "Smart-Shift" transmissions. Those transmissions allow operators to choose between three different shifting options, including manual shift, automatic shift through gears one to four, and automatic shift through gears two to four. Buyers can choose from a long line of options and special features, including a number of different tire sizes and styles. Or consider the fact that Deere offers an extra-special attachment that can work on its 444H, 544H, and 624H loaders—tool carriers. To get a complete list of current John Deere loaders, and to learn about the advantages of the various different models, please visit your local John Deere industrial dealer. With as many options as Deere has for those machines, in addition to the already-impressive list of standard-equipment features for them, you'll be glad you did.

Landscape Loaders

For quite some time, the only landscape loader in Deere & Company's line has been the Model 210LE. This model is highly productive both with its front-end loader and its three-point hitch. The most common attachment fitted onto the 210LE's hitch is a box blade, which is very handy for

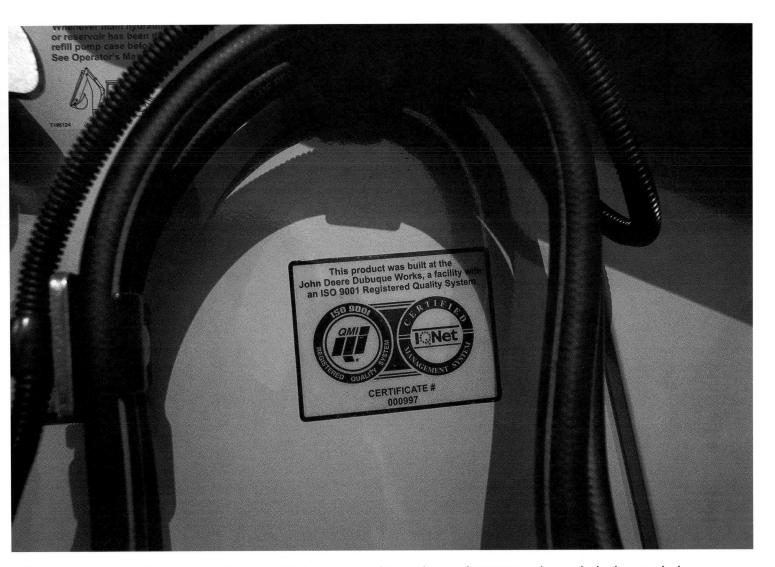

Both Deere & Company's Dubuque Works and Davenport Works are registered in compliance with ISO 9001 quality standards. Those standards are internationally recognized, and Deere's compliance is further evidence of the company's excellence.

most landscaping and land-leveling jobs. And the 210LE landscape loader has plenty of power, too. Its four-cylinder, 276-ci engine produces an advertised 73 SAE net horsepower, plenty of power to do the jobs such a tractor needs to do.

Skid Steer Loaders

In recent years, John Deere skid steer loaders have caught the attention of many different people, and for good reason. The current line of skid steers includes the Models 240, 250, 260, and 270. All of these models, which range from the 53-horsepower Model 240 to the 77-horsepower Model 270, feature great visibility and a special vertical-lift system that helps give them superior performance.

Deere has also made these machines all the more versatile with a long line of "Worksite Pro" attachments. They include multi-purpose buckets and a wide variety of specialized buckets, for construction, materials, foundry work, and more. The special lineup of attachments includes much more than just buckets. It also features backhoes, augers, power rakes, pallet forks, bale spears, rotary tillers, trenchers, rollers, cold planers, breakers (otherwise known as jackhammers), and even more. Yet

One could argue that modern John Deere industrials don't just perform better than their predecessors, but they are also nicer looking. It seems obvious that Deere remains dedicated to producing high-quality machines that are both easy on operator's bodies and easy on the eyes of almost everyone that looks at the units.

Bearing the name "DEERE" on its engine side cover, this big Model 644H John Deere loader has labeling like that common on Deere's more recent loaders. Many of Deere's current industrial machines, loaders like this one included, also feature curved lines that not only make the machines more eye-appealing but also often help give the operator a clearer view of the job at hand.

another special Worksite Pro attachment is a set of tracks. Overall, John Deere skid steer loaders are superb performers.

Scrapers: Moving Dirt

Tracing their roots back to the Model 762A and Model 862A scrapers that made their debut in 1980, the Model 762B and Model 862B scrapers came out in the 1985 model year. The two models had a long run but eventually were replaced with improved versions. Dubbed the Model 762B and 862B Series II scrapers, these units both featured large-capacity bowls— 11.5-cubic-yard heaped capacity for the 762B and 17-cubic-yard heaped

capacity for the 862B. Both scrapers also featured large fuel tanks, the 762B holding 87 gallons and its bigger brother 100 gallons. The scrapers also had a long list of special standard-equipment features that made them appealing to many customers, including a special chain design that prolonged the life of that component, a load-sensing hydraulic pump, a stout engine, and numerous operator conveniences, including an adjustable steering wheel.

Interestingly, Deere & Company made a move in its scraper production that, in a way, calls to mind the days of the Model 830-I industrial tractors fitted with

The John Deere Model 210LE landscape loader features a 4-cylinder engine and a four-speed transmission, which provides four speeds both forward and in reverse. Though small compared to many Deere industrial machines, this unit does its job well.

For quite some time, the Model 210LE has been Deere & Company's only landscape loader. The 210LE is just the right size for most landscaping work, but it's not just used to help make lawns look more attractive. This unit, for instance, has found employment on a highway construction project on what used to be Route 66.

Hancock scrapers. Deere decided that it could manufacture specialized pull-type scrapers for use with its larger-horsepower tractors (ranging from 225 to 450 horsepower) that would in most cases perform as well as, if not better than, the full-fledged scraper units like the 762B and 862B.

Today, Deere & Company has three pull-type scrapers in its product line. The Model 1412E scraper can be pulled with Deere's 225-horsepower tractors, whereas the larger Models 1810E and 1814E are designed for use with Deere's modern four-wheel-drive tractors.

Excavators

Ever since the introduction of the Model JD690 excavator back in 1969, Deere & Company has been heavily involved in the production of these powerful machines. Thirty years later, the company has an impressive lineup of at least 11 excavator models (excluding the small compact ZTS series excavators). Those 11 models range from the small Model 80 excavator, weighing in at less than 4 tons, to the enormous Model 750 excavator, tipping the scales at more than 82 tons.

Back in 1988, Deere & Company teamed up with Hitachi in the manufacturing of excavators and other industrial machines. The joint venture expanded the product lines of both companies, giving

This recent lineup of skid steer loaders at a John Deere industrial dealer in Oklahoma City gives a pretty good indication of how popular the machines are. In 2001, Deere's skid steer line included four different models offering a wide range of power, available features, and attachments.

Deere an increased number of excavator models.

Compact Excavators

When the going gets tough and there isn't much wiggle room, sometimes the right answer isn't bigger, it's smaller. Deere's compact excavators—the Models 17ZTS, 27ZTS, 35ZTS, and 50ZTS—belong to a very special excavator series. The ZTS series compact excavators feature Deere's "Zero Tail Swing" design, which lets the units spin around a full 360 degrees without having to worry about hanging or banging the tail of the unit on obstructions in tight quarters.

Again, Deere wasn't content with letting the compact excavators just excavate by digging holes. The company equipped the ZTS series units with a backfill blade so that they could fill the holes they made with ease. The blade also gives the units an extra bit of stability in certain situations. Furthermore, Deere & Company made a variety of "Work-site Pro" attachments. They include hydraulic hammers, hydraulic augers, quick-coupler rakes, and a variety of special buckets.

Motor Graders

Ever since Deere's introduction of the revolutionary Model JD570 motor grader in 1967, the company has been heavily involved in producing innovative road graders. Recent models include the Models 670C, 670CH, 672CH, 770C, 770CH, and the 772CH. The 672CH and 772CH models feature a unique system of all-wheel-drive

By virtue of their design and intent, most skid steer loaders are fairly compact machines. Thus, the operator's station in a skid steer is usually also fairly compact. Yet Deere & Company's skid steers have many features that provide comfort, convenience, and increased safety for the operator.

"continuous-feedback" control that adjusts the speed of the front wheels as conditions require.

Dozers: Pushing When They Need To

Ever since Deere started producing its own Model MC crawlers back in 1949, Deere & Company has been well known for bulldozers.

The Models 762B and 862B Series II served as Deere's last self-powered scrapers. Since they were discontinued around the turn of the twenty-first century, Deere has been selling only pull-type scrapers to fill that market's needs.

Deere's hydraulic excavator line includes several models that collectively cover a broad horsepower range. Many of those models can also be fitted with special dipper sticks (otherwise known as arms) that increase the depth to which these machines can dig.

Were it not for the advent of the crawler tractor and bulldozer, hydraulic excavators may not have become as popular for industrial customers as they have. These units typically ride on tracks, which help give them solid footing. Rubber tires aren't quite as effective because they "give" more than tracks do.

Compared to most industrial machines — except for skid steers and John Deere's Gators — Deere's compact excavators look tiny. The machines nevertheless have a lot of heart and are, by virtue of their size, more nimble than most industrial machines.

The company offers a long line of dozer models with an impressive array of features and options. For instance, Deere has made several of its bulldozers available with a number of different undercarriage/track types. These at least include "regular" models, low-ground pressure models, long-track models, wide-track models, and even wide-extra-long-track models. In 2001, Deere's dozer lineup included models ranging from the 70-horsepower, 15,000-pound Model 450H with a 97-inch blade, to the gargantuan 1050C, a dozer that provided an impressive 324 horsepower, wielded a 165-inch blade, and tipped the scales at around 74,000 pounds, according to Deere literature for the models.

Deere's ZTS series compact excavators feature a special curved back end that is far more important than some people might first realize. That curved back end makes it possible for operators to run the machines without having to worry about possibly slamming the back end of it into something in the middle of a turn.

Forklifts

The current John Deere fork-lifts—the Models 485E, 486E, and 488E—are in many ways very similar to each other. The most noticeable difference among the models—all of which are available in either two- or four-wheel-drive versions—is their lift capacities, which correspond directly with the last number of each model's designation. For instance, the Model 485E has a 5,000-pound lift capacity at ground level, the Model 486E has a 6,000-pound capacity, and the Model 488E an 8,000-pound lift capacity. The masts on those forklifts can tilt forward as much as 30 degrees from vertical and can tilt backward as much as 10 degrees from vertical.

Deere's Forestry Machines

Deere & Company today serves as one of the largest producers of machines for forestry work. Included in the lineup are log loaders, skidders, feller bunchers, delimbers, and even more. Those machines represent a special part of Deere's industrial division and have their roots back in the early John Deere crawlers that first started earning their keep in the forests some five decades ago.

The John Deere "Gators"

One of the biggest headlines for Deere in the 1990s was its introduction of the John Deere "Gator." Although it is likened by some to a golf cart, the Gator is a far more powerful and versatile utility vehicle. And, what's more, John Deere

Compact excavators can dig holes and trenches just like their bigger brothers can, except the compacts do so on a smaller scale. Also, just like their bigger brothers, Deere's compact excavators offer their operators tremendous visibility.

One thing that Deere's compact excavators have that isn't typically found on the full-size, much larger hydraulic excavators is the backfilling blade. Often these small excavators need to refill the holes they just dug, so this feature allows the same machine to do both jobs — similar to the way a backhoe loader can be used for backfilling.

Very noticeable with its bright yellow paint scheme, this John Deere tractor is great for roadside duty, including mowing. Hydraulics, lighting, great visibility, air conditioning, numerous other operator conveniences, even more great features, and John Deere quality all help make this unit as great as it is.

Note that this mower tractor features side-view mirrors, which enable the operator to keep tabs on the trailing mower. A variety of other John Deere industrial tractors are also available with mirrors.

In 2001, Deere & Company had as many as six motor grader models in production. These machines have become increasingly popular over the years, and they aren't just used to grade country roads. Indeed, many of these machines find their way onto construction sites as well.

Even though Deere's industrial tractor production began with a wheel tractor, crawler tractors deserve a lot of credit for helping Deere achieve success in industrial tractor production. Dating back to the D Lindemans and the BO Lindemans, crawlers have almost always been important, if not essential, to the company's industrial production. Today's full-fledged, highly advanced John Deere bulldozers remain important to Deere in that regard, even though the company now has many other industrial machines that have a convincing hold on the market.

now offers a specialized version of the Gator called the Worksite Gator. While most John Deere Gators feature green and yellow paint, the Worksite Gator features a yellow paint scheme appropriate for most industrial applications. Powered by a three-cylinder Yanmar diesel engine, the Worksite Gator is rated at 18 horsepower, can haul as much as 1,400 pounds (including the weight of the operator and passenger), and can pull an additional 1,400 pounds.

Like so many of Deere's other industrial products, the John Deere Gator and the John Deere Worksite Gator are available with a wide variety of options and attachments. The Worksite Gator comes standard fitted with many of the items that are optional on the other Gator models. These features include an electric lift kit, a heavy-duty suspension kit, chain guards, tie-down rings, bedliner, brush guards, and more. Optional on the Worksite Gator are things such as an electric winch kit, a power lift kit, a tool holder, a 72-inch front blade, a 50-gallon sprayer, windshield, and a variety of equipment used for sporting events—things such as a ball field finisher, a line marker, and the "Med-Bed" for medical rescues. Many traditional Gators

The owner of this 1980s model John Deere 750 bulldozer seems very pleased with the performance of the unit. The hydrostatic drive, which this bulldozer (and many other bulldozers) came with, makes handling these machines a dream compared to earlier units.

The number of bulldozers Deere & Company offers today is quite astounding. In 2001, for instance, the company had as many as 17 advertised crawler dozer models in production (including specialized models). That number included, among others, Deere's LGP (low ground pressure) and LT (long track) models.

Many different branches of industry find John Deere forklifts quite useful. Indeed, even though most people think forklifts are simply used to move pallets in warehouses or factories, they can also be used to lift and move a variety of other kinds of materials. Some people even use the model to help paint buildings (using the forklift as a kind of scaffolding) or to lift materials up to rooftops, among other things.

This modern John Deere forklift proudly bears the name "DEERE" in striking white letters with black outlining. Earlier Deere & Company industrial machines bore simple, solid black letters on the industrial yellow tractors, but today's trademark name jumps out even better in the form seen here. On construction sites throughout the world, people will see the word "DEERE" on thousands of Deere industrial machines, assuring the onlookers that those construction sites are in good hands.

The logo seen here has likely appeared on more industrial and agricultural tractors than any other Deere & Company trademark logo. Still a sign of excellence, this logo has been replaced, though, with a more futuristic logo, one that continues to speak of excellence but also helps to show Deere & Company's innovative, highly technological side.

find themselves working in industrial jobs as well, oftentimes being fitted with a variety of different attachments or accessories.

ADTs: Articulated Dump Trucks

In 1999, Deere & Company teamed up with the Bell Equipment Company of Richards Bay, South Africa. This arrangement gave Deere the distribution rights for Bell's articulated dump trucks (also known as ADTs), a product never before seen in the John Deere line. ADTs feature articulated frames that make the enormous machines much more maneuverable than appearances suggest.

Deere's line of ADTs includes four different models, and even the smallest one is big. That ADT, the Model 250C, is the only Deere model powered by an in-line six-cylinder turbocharged Daimler-Chrysler engine. All of the other Deere ADTs—the Models 300C, 350C, and 400C—are powered by Mercedes-Benz V8 engines. The models produce tremendous horsepower, ranging from the 250C with its advertised 237 SAE net horsepower to the 400C with 410 SAE net horsepower. And with that horsepower comes the ability to carry large loads. Deere advertises that the Model 250C ADT has a heaped-load capacity of 18 cubic yards, while the big Model 400C can carry up to 29 cubic yards heaped. According to Deere documents, the model designations of its ADTs reflect the rated payload for the units. For instance, the Model 300C has a rated payload of

Deere & Company's articulated dump trucks, more popularly known as ADTs, are immense units. For instance, the smaller Model 250C tips the scales at more than 36,000 pounds unloaded, according to Deere literature. Loaded, that model can weigh slightly more than 87,000 pounds.

The John Deere "Gator" units have seen a tremendous increase in popularity in recent years. For instance, many colleges use these units for grounds maintenance, sporting events, and more. This unit—seen here in front of Southwestern Oklahoma State University's oldest building, the "Old Science building"—can be seen working almost daily.

slightly less than 30 tons, whereas the 350C is rated at about 35 tons.

Another notable feature of Deere's ADTs is the wide range of speeds at which the units can travel. For instance, the 250C has six forward speeds ranging from 4 to 30 miles per hour, while its biggest brother—the 400C—features a dual-range transmission with five gears, giving the model 10 forward speeds ranging from 2.5 to 30 miles per hour.

The John Deere articulated dump trucks are certainly stout machines that do their jobs well.

A New Name for Deere's Industrial Division

In July 2001, Deere & Company announced that it had changed the name of what had been the company's Construction Equipment Division. The new name—the Worldwide Construction and Forestry Division—better reflects the company's increased involvement worldwide in both construction and forestry equipment.

Deere & Company has a long history of producing industrial tractors and machines, and the company looks well prepared to make even greater moves in those fields in the years to come. And considering the reliability and versatility of John Deere products, it's likely that many of the John Deere industrials of today will still be in use many years from now.

DEERE TRADEMARK LOGO CORNER:
DEERE REVEALS A NEW TRADEMARK LOGO IN 2000

Way back in 1968, Deere & Company decided to change its trademark logo. That logo had found itself on new John Deere products for approximately 32 years, and it became the quickest way to distinguish Deere machines from the rest. Like all other Deere trademark logos, the 1968 version came to represent quality products. Thirty-two years later, Deere's new trademark logo still stands as a mark of high quality.

For the year 2000—a notable year for many reasons—Deere unveiled a new trademark logo. It was the first featuring the familiar John Deere deer at the start of a jump, with its hind legs still on the ground, rather than in the air and preparing for a landing—perhaps suggesting that Deere is well grounded, but always reaching for higher accomplishments in the future. The new logo gives off a bolder, stronger, more high-tech feeling than previous Deere trademarks.

Despite their size, Deere ADTs are far more maneuverable than they initially would appear to be. Their articulated frame makes these big machines turn tighter than they likely would be able to with conventional steering.

INDEX

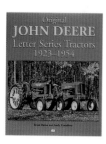

**Original John Deere Letter Series
Tractors 1923–1954**
ISBN 0-7603-0912-4

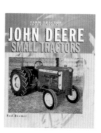

John Deere Small Tractors
ISBN 0-7603-1130-7

**Inside John Deere:
A Factory History**
ISBN 0-7603-0441-6

John Deere Farm Tractors
ISBN 0-87938-755-6

John Deere New Generation Tractors
ISBN 0-7603-0427-0

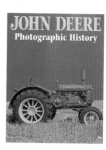

John Deere Photographic History
ISBN 0-7603-0058-5

Farm Tractor Milestones
ISBN 0-7603-0730-X

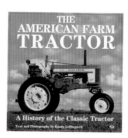

The American Farm Tractor
ISBN 0-7603-1370-9

The American Barn
ISBN 0-7603-0109-3

Find us on the internet at www.motorbooks.com   1-800-826-6600